New Images of the Last Things

Karl Rahner on Death and Life After Death

MARIE MURPHY

Paulist Press
New York / Mahwah, N.J.

Acknowledgments
Materials reprinted in *New Images of the Last Things* first appeared in the following publications and are reprinted with permission: Quotes from *A Rahner Reader* by Gerald A. McCool, pp. 73, 361, Seabury Press, N.Y.; "Particular Judgment," *Sacramentum Mundi*, Vol. 3 by Karl Rahner, p. 275, Seabury Press, N.Y.; "The Christian Faith," in *Doctrinal Documents of the Catholic Church* by J. Neuner, S.J. and J. Depuis, S.J., 1982, p. 138, Seabury Press, N.Y.; "A World of Grace," 1980, from *Hope for Humanity: Rahner's Eschatology* by William Thompson, Editor Leo J. O'Donovan, p. 112, Seabury Press, N.Y.; *The Foundations of the Christian Faith* (1978) by Karl Rahner, trans. by William V. Dyck, p. 433, Seabury Press, N.Y.; "Marxist Utopia and the Christian Future of Man," *Theological Investigations*, Vol. 6, by Karl Rahner, p. 60, Seabury Press, N.Y.; Scripture selections taken from *The New American Bible With Revised New Testament*, copyright © 1986 by the Confraternity of Christian Doctrine, Washington, D.C.; Quotations from *The Documents of Vatican II*, Abbott-Gallagher edition are reprinted with the permission of America Press, Inc., 106 West 56th St. N.Y., N.Y. 10019, 1966. All rights reserved; *Everlasting Life After Death* (1976) by E.J. Fortman, S.J., pp. 110, 132, 133 by Alba House, N.Y.; *The Puritan Way of Death* by David E. Stannard, Oxford University Press; *The Way of the Lord Jesus Christ* by Germain Grisez, Franciscan Herald Press. The English translation of the Easter Proclamation (exsultet) from the *Rite of Holy Week* © 1970, International Committee on English in the Liturgy, Inc. All rights reserved; Excerpts from *Sharing the Light of Faith*, *Economic Justice for All*, *The Challenge of Peace: God's Promise and our Response* published by the United States Catholic Conference; *Encounters with Silence* (1984) by Karl Rahner, pp. 81–87 (passim), Maryland Christian Classics; *God and the New Physics* (1983) by Paul Davier, p. 3 by Simon and Schuster N.Y.; from *Gilgamesh* by Herbert Mason. Copyright © 1970 by Herbert Mason, Houghton Mifflin Company.

Book design by Nighthawk Design.

Library of Congress Cataloging-in-Publication Data

Murphy, Marie.
    New images of the last things : Karl Rahner on death and life after death / Marie Murphy.
        p.   cm.
    Includes bibliographies.
    ISBN 0-8091-3052-1 : $6.95
    1. Eschatology—History of doctrines—20th century. 2. Death—Religious aspects—Catholic Church—History of doctrines—20th century. 3. Future life—Catholic Church—History of doctrines—20th century. 4. Catholic Church—Doctrines—History—20th century. 5. Rahner, Karl, 1904– . I. Title.
BT819.5.M83   1989
236—dc19   88-37963
                                                                      CIP

Published by Paulist Press
997 Macarthur Boulevard
Mahwah, New Jersey 07430

Printed and bound in the
United States of America

Contents

Death and Dying

Gilgamesh was King of Uruk
a city set between the Tigris
and Euphrates rivers
in Ancient Babylonia.
Enkidu was born on the steppe
where he grew up among the animals.
Gilgamesh was called a god and man.
Enkidu was animal and man.
This is the story of their becoming
human together.

(When Enkidu was killed, Gilgamesh . . .)
Perhaps insane he tried to bring
Enkidu back to life,
to end his bitterness
His fear of death,
His life became a quest

to find the secret of eternal life
Which he might carry back to give his friend.

(Gilgamesh goes to see Utnapishtim
who lives across the sea of death
and asks . . .)
Is there something more than death?
Some other end to friendship?
I came crossed the mountains and the sea.
(Utnapishtim, moved by the grief of Gilgamesh shows him where
    to find the plant of life which assures immortality, but on his

way back across the sea of death, the plant is snatched from
Gilgamesh by a sea serpent who devours it. And so Gilgamesh
laments . . .)
Is there something more than death?
Some other end to friendship?[1]

Since the beginning of human history all human beings
have sought the answer to the question: Why must we die and
what happens to us when we do? Beginning with the first
written record of man's experience of death, *The Epic of
Gilgamesh*, we find in sources from antiquity to the contemporary era evidence of humankind's quest to understand the
human journey after death.

It is never an easy thing to speak of death and dying. The
loss of those we love haunts us, and the possibility of our own
death seems absurd or terrifying. Psychologists tell us that
the thought of our own mortality is so impossible for us to
accept that we literally cannot imagine ourselves dead. Even
when we picture what our death will be like, we somehow
imagine ourselves hovering near our mourning family and
friends.

Yet today death is becoming an increasingly popular topic
of conversation. Death, which was once considered taboo to
be spoken of, is now examined and explained in articles,
books, and TV documentaries. Why this interest in death?

One of the reasons may be that recent medical progress has
raised many questions about death and dying. The ability to
sustain life by medical techniques has raised serious ethical
questions about when life stops and death begins. So too,
progress in the area of resuscitation, that is bringing patients
"back to life" who have been pronounced dead, has created
interest in some patients' reports of their near-death experiences. Many patients report remarkably similar experiences
of being outside of one's body.

In the twentieth century there is also global concern with

death and dying. The contemporary person not only ponders the meaning of his/her own existence, but too many wars and too much destruction have brought humankind to the brink of an abyss over which we not only ponder the meaning of our own life but also are haunted by the menace of the possible annihilation of the whole human race.

"Does life make sense?" We may wonder. We cannot answer this question unless we also can answer the question, "Does death make sense?" For what we believe about death reveals our attitudes about life, the nature of being human, and the world.

Our Christian faith teaches that death is the end of our pilgrimage toward God, an event in which we hope that by letting go of our earthly lives we enter into a different manner of existence.

But while the modern person seems more willing than ever to examine the question of death, contemporary interest in a far-away heavenly kingdom appears to be waning. Never before have human beings been so concerned with the state of human life on earth. Ignoring or enduring conditions which exist in today's world in the hope of one day making up for it in heaven is not acceptable anymore. Heavenly promises which are no earthly good are rejected in today's world.

Humankind has entered into a new phase in its history. Never before has the human race been so aware of its relationship with the world and the universe. New discoveries in science, physics, and psychology have raised questions about the nature of reality and our relationship with the material order, that is the world and the universe. Scientists tell us that we are part of a universe which is an intimately interrelated system. Each one of us is an indispensable part of the earth, the sun, and the stars.

These discoveries call into question many of the traditional ways in which death and dying have been understood. The church has many teachings about what happens at and after death. These teachings about the "last things" are called *eschatological* teachings. In the Christian tradition death has been understood as the separation of the soul from the body. The church has taught that at death each person is judged, rewarded, or condemned to heaven, hell or purgatory, there to wait for the second coming of Christ, the resurrection of the body, and the final consummation of the world.

Are these images of death, such as the soul separating from the body, purgatory as a painful, if temporary, place of atonement, resurrection as a resuscitation of our present physical bodies, and the second coming of Christ as a specific event which will take place on a predictable day, compatible with the present human understanding of who we are and what the world is?

What really are the teachings of the church about death and dying and what do they have to do with the person in the world today?

Karl Rahner

On March 30, 1984, the world mourned the passing of Karl Rahner, internationally known as an eminent scholar, a prolific writer, a loyal member of the Society of Jesus, a servant of the church and the most pastoral of men.

Rahner's pastoral concern was to present the Christian message in a way that was understandable to persons in today's world. While he held that the basic faith content of the doctrinal teachings of the church remains constant, he also maintained that these doctrinal teachings must be questioned anew by each age so that they are meaningful for persons today.

Rahner was particularly concerned with the teachings of the church on death and life after death. Rahner thought that the eschatological teachings of the church (the teachings on death and life after death) were presented in images which were not meaningful to the contemporary person. He felt that the idea of an afterlife which was completely separated from or at odds with this world was not compatible with our present understanding of our relationship with the world and the universe. In today's world Rahner has said that we are "children of the earth" and because of this the modern person must be profoundly materialistic.

Rahner proposes a new understanding of the relationship of the human being with the world and the universe. He suggests that the human person maintains a lasting relationship with the world and the universe even in death.

Furthermore, Rahner holds that by the death and resurrection of Jesus Christ, the universe and the world have already been radically transformed. Christ has become part of the world and the universe.

In order to understand what Rahner means, this study begins by examining Rahner's understanding of the human person and the person's relationship to the world. We will then be better able to understand Rahner's theology of death and the last things.

What is it that makes us human beings? Human beings, unlike inanimate objects, can know, think, feel, and choose. Rahner begins his study of what it means to be a human being by examining how a person knows. All human beings receive information through their senses. We see, hear, touch, taste, or smell something. Rahner held that there is a system of ordering information received from the senses in the mind. We receive sense impressions. Our mind places them in categories. We form an image of what we are seeing or hearing in our minds and we form ideas and concepts.

Rahner gave credit to Immanuel Kant for determining that there were conditions in the knowing person which made knowledge possible.[2] Immanuel Kant (1724–1804), a French philosopher, taught that the way a human person knows the world is shaped by the mind of the person. We literally do see and understand the world through different eyes and in different ways.

Like Kant, Rahner holds that the human person knows by a structure which is part of the mind. But unlike Kant who held that human beings can know only that which they experience through their senses, Rahner believes that in forming concepts and ideas, human beings are capable of reaching out to that which cannot be seen or touched.[3]

Rahner says that in each human being there is a longing for the infinite, for the more which our senses cannot grasp. Rahner calls this drive within all human beings the *vorgriff*. It is a dynamic drive that reaches out for the infinite.

Rahner says that in knowing not only does every human being experience that there is more to life than what we experience with our senses. Rahner also says that it is in the act of knowing other persons and other things that human beings know themselves. In knowing objects, the person realizes that he is not the object. He is different from the object. The newborn baby looks at and touches the mobile above his crib. Eventually he realizes that he is not the mobile. He is different from it. He is the one thinking, touching, and looking. Everything else is that which is not himself.

Human beings experience themselves only by experiencing what is different from themselves.[4]

Therefore, in every act of knowing a person knows himself, and, according to Rahner, in every act of knowing a person consciously or not experiences God.

Human beings experience God in knowing because the more that we long for, the infinite horizon for which our hearts are always restless as Augustine said, is none other than God.

Rahner held that not only do we come to know God and ourselves by experiencing other persons and objects; he also believed that there was an important and lasting relationship between persons and material things. We came to know who we are because we experience the world outside us. At the same time the world outside us is conditioned by our minds. It is only human minds which give an intelligent framework to the world and the universe. Human beings alone make sense out of the earth, the sun, and the stars!

Therefore, says Rahner, human beings must be forever an-

chored in material things.[5] Without the world and universe
we cannot know ourselves or God!

Human beings are made of and know themselves through
matter. But human beings are also spirit. We are anchored in
matter, in the real things of the earth and the universe, but
that part of us which longs for God—for being without
limits—is spirit. We long to be freed from our limits and to
lose ourselves in mystery. We long to go out of ourselves.

Rahner cautions that while the human spirit longs for and
is capable of reaching out into that which is beyond us and
spiritual, human beings are *finite* spirits.[6] Human beings cannot exist without matter. Rahner prefers to speak of the human person as being made up of matter and spirit rather than
body and soul. It is the essence of being human to be matter
and spirit—even in death. We will see that this position is
very important in Rahner's understanding of death. How can
we say that in death the soul is separated from the body, if
according to Rahner a person is spirit–matter and the spirit
can never be separated from matter?

Rahner's understanding of what a human being is cannot
be understood without considering Rahner's interpretation of
how human beings are free because they have the power to
decide about themselves. But freedom should not be thought
of as the ability to make many decisions; the heart of human
freedom is the desire to make a final decision for God. Rahner
holds that all human beings long for God whether or not we
call what we long for "God." Our hearts long to give ourselves
in complete surrender to the one who is above and beyond us
infinitely and yet calls us by name. According to Rahner, human beings can only achieve this total surrender to God in
death.[7]

Death

According to Karl Rahner, the last words of Jesus on the
cross, "My God, my God, why have you abandoned me?" and

"Father, into your hands I commend my spirit," express what is most horrible and what is most wonderful about death.[8]

Rahner believes that we actually hunger for death and would dread everlasting life as we know it now. He says, "If anyone were to tell us that the state we had lived in up to now would simply continue on into eternity, in that self-same moment we would have to recognize ourselves as dammed."[9] Human beings long for completion. We want to achieve a definite end. Death is that act in which a person gathers up his/her whole life and all that he/she is and says, "Here I am, Lord!"

In death, the human being is freed from all limits of time and space and becomes radically free.[10] In death the whole life of a person is finalized, fulfilled, and brought into the presence of God.

Death is a decision. In death, human beings decide finally and totally for God or against God.[11] There are two aspects of death though. Death is experienced actively and passively. Death is experienced actively since it is the final act of a person's life. In death, a person sums up all that he or she has been in life. But death must also be experienced passively. Death is that absolute darkness which no human being can control or manipulate. In death all human beings must accept their own powerlessness. In death we are deprived of everything and robbed completely of control over overselves.[12]. In this sense, death is absurd. It is the arch-contradiction of life. In death everything is taken away from us. Human beings rightly fear death. The pain and suffering associated with death is a consequence of sin. Because of Adam's sin, humankind experiences death as the death of a sinner.[13]

Rahner states that he does not mean that if Adam had not sinned, human beings would never have died. He says, though, that death would have been experienced without fear or suffering. The experience of death as darkness and fear is the result of Adam's sin.[14]

Death can only be understood correctly when it is understood in the light of Christ's death.[15] In becoming human,

Christ assumed the whole of our existence including our human experience of the darkness of death. From the distance of two thousand years it often seems that the cross of Christ has been made into a throne. We have so often imagined Christ on his cross planning the resurrection Sunday reunion with his friends. We do not dare to remember that he hung there in the darkness as the powers of hell assaulted him.

Christ accepted the total powerlessness and self-surrender of death. He abandoned himself to that mystery which waited in the darkness.

Through his death, Christ transformed human dying which had been a manifestation of sin into a manifestation of grace.[16]

Rahner is not saying, however, that by his death Christ "paid for our sins," as he disagrees with the theory that sees the death of Christ as satisfaction for sin. This understanding of Christ's death emphasizes the necessity of an infinite satisfaction due to God for man's offense. Since man sinned against an infinite God, man as a finite being is forever incapable of achieving satisfaction. Only Christ, whose acts are of infinite value because he is both God and man is capable of achieving satisfaction. Thus, the death of Christ made infinite satisfaction to God for the sin of finite man.[17]

Rahner holds that this theory neglects the true understanding of Christ's life and death. According to Rahner, the whole of Christ's life must be viewed from the perspective of his death. In his death, Christ summed up in a definitive act the totality of his person and his freedom.[18]

> The real miracle of Christ's death resides precisely in this: death, which can be experienced only as the advent of emptiness, as the dead-end of sin, as the darkness of eternal night . . . and which could be suffered, even by Christ himself, only as a state of being abandoned by God, now, through being embraced by the obedient "yes" of the Son, while losing nothing of the horror of divine abandonment native to death, is transformed into something completely different! into the advent of

God in the midst of that empty loneliness into the manifestation of a complete surrender of the whole man to the Holy God
at the very moment when man seems lost and far removed
from him.[19]

In his death, Christ experienced all that we humans experience in the darkness of death: emptiness, powerlessness, re-
moteness from God, the bitterness of guilt.[20] At the fullness of
that moment when all seemed lost and God truly removed
from him, Christ cried out, "My God, my God, why have you
abandoned me?"

In death, Christ in the definitive act of his whole person
and his reality as the word of God said yes to the incomprehensible mystery of God. "Father, into your hands I commend my
spirit."

Rahner's understanding of death, then, has serious implications for our understanding of our own death. The death of
Christ has made what was darkness light. His death has made
what was an expression of sin into an expression of God's
presence.

In considering our own death, we, like Christ, must not
imagine it to be a single act or event at the end of life, but we
must conceive of our death as the definite and final expression
of all that is valuable and meant to be about us. Death is the
assent in freedom to the mystery of God.

Our contemporary society often attempts to either glamor-
ize death or to deny its more painful aspects. Rahner reminds
us that since it is part of our human nature to surrender to
God, the refusal to surrender oneself in death can be a mortal
sin. In refusing to say yes to God and attempting to maintain
our self-control, death may be an act of negation—a no to all
that we were meant to be.

The surrender of self is not easy, and Rahner's emphasis on
the agony, emptiness, and solitude of Christ's' surrender
make us painfully aware of this. "My God, my God, why have
you abandoned me?"

But the death of Christ also illustrates for us another key

aspect of Rahner's theology of death. Christ in his humanity dies in hope. The death of Christ on the cross illustrates hope in what seems impossible. "Father, into your hands I commend my spirit."

Rahner's theology of death does not give us assurances and guarantees concerning the outcome of death, but simply hope. We dare to hope that in the face of total surrender, we are not surrendering to chaos or emptiness. Death is surrender to an infinite person who calls us by name. We, too, dare to say, "Father, into your hands I commend my spirit."

We see then that human beings are quite literally born to die. Rahner understands that in the act of knowing, human beings not only come to know themselves and the world but also experiences a drive toward that which is incomprehensible and mysterious. Everything in our human nature longs to reach out and surrender to this unseen mystery. This complete and total surrender of ourselves is possible only when we say yes to death. But then what happens to us when we do?

NOTES

1. Herbert Mason, *Gilgamesh, A Verse Narrative* (New York: New American Library, 1972), p. 15.

2. Karl Rahner, "Eternity from Time," *The Practice of Faith* (New York: Crossroad, 1983), p. 305.

3. Karl Rahner, *The Foundations of the Christian Faith*, trans. William V. Dych (New York: Seabury Press, 1978), p. 20.

4. Karl Rahner, *Spirit in the World* (New York: Herder and Herder, 1968), p. 383.

5. Karl Rahner, "Reflections on Methodology in Theology," *Theological Investigations*, Vol. 11 (Baltimore: Helicon Press, 1961), p. 88.

6. Rahner, *Spirit in the World*, p. 383.

7. Karl Rahner, "On Christian Dying," *Theological Investigations*, Vol. 7, trans. David Bourke (New York: Herder and Herder, 1971), p. 287.

8. Karl Rahner, *On the Theology of Death*, trans. Charles H. Henkey (New York: Herder and Herder, 1971), p. 87.

9. Karl Rahner, "Theological Considerations Concerning the Moment of Death," *Theological Investigations*, Vol. 11, p. 320.

10. Rahner, "Theological Observations on the Concept of Time," *Theological Investigations*, Vol. 11, p. 288. Rahner conceives of time and eternity in terms of freedom. He believes that we are tyrannized by our concept of time so that we think of life after death as a continuation of events in a linear fashion. According to Rahner, death radically removes us from time.

11. Rahner, "On Christian Dying," *Theological Investigations*, Vol. 7, p. 290.

12. Karl Rahner, "The Universality of Salvation," *Theological Investigations*, Vol. 16, trans. David Morland (London: Darton, Longman & Todd, 1979), p. 224.

13. Rahner, *On the Theology of Death*, p. 56.

14. Ibid., p. 42.

15. Ibid., p. 65.

16. Ibid., p. 69.

17. Ibid., p. 66.

18. Ibid., p. 70.

19. Ibid., p. 78.

2

The All-Cosmic Dimension of the Soul

W e have seen that the experience of the darkness and fear of death is the result of sin.[1] In fact, human beings long for death as total fulfillment. This fulfillment, says Rahner, must include the perfection of the body. Human perfection which does not include the body is unnatural and impossible.[2]

Traditionally, when we have thought of death, we have understood death as the separation of the soul from the body. In death the soul departs from and becomes unrelated to the world. The soul exists in a dimension that has nothing to do with the world and the universe; Rahner points out that in western society we tend to think that there is a direct ratio between nearness to God and the lack of relation to the world. "Be holy, don't be worldly," we may have been told. Therefore, death must mean being entirely removed from the world so that we might be in the presence of God.

In response to this interpretation of death, Rahner raises the question of the unity of the body and the soul. He states that the image of the soul "escaping from the body" is not found in the Bible and is not part of the teaching of the church.[3]

Rahner points out that the soul is the *form* of the body. The soul is that which gives the body life. The soul and body are forever united. The soul cannot be a soul without a body. Yet anyone who has ever seen a corpse knows that something has left the body. The "person" is no longer there. How then can the soul exist after its separation from the body?

Rahner proposes a new understanding of the unity of the body and soul which he calls the *all-cosmic dimension*.[4] He says that while in death the soul ends its present relationship with a particular physical body, it continues a relationship with the world and the universe.

> With the . . . termination of her (the soul's present relation to the body . . . her entrance into some deeper, all embracing openness (occurs) in which her cosmic relationship to the universe is more fully realized.[5]

According to Rahner, it is never possible for the soul to exist in a completely non-material way. Rahner does not accept the image of souls separated from their bodies that are awaiting reunion with that body at the end of the world. Rahner explained that through its entrance in death into an all-cosmic dimension, the world and the universe became, so to speak, the body of the soul.

Rahner cautions that he does not mean that the world becomes the body of the soul as the physical body was during life. The all-cosmic relationship means that the soul enters into a new relationship with the world and the universe. In Rahner's thought it is our limited understanding of what we mean by "body" which keeps us from understanding the all-cosmic dimension of the soul. In time and space, human beings express themselves through their physical bodies during life. Our bodies show who we are, and what we feel and think. But our physical bodies are also limited by time and space. Our hearts may fly to the moon, but our physical body will not without the help of a spacecraft.

In death, human beings are freed from the physical limits of the body and enter into a new relationship with the world. Rahner notes that we should not limit our understanding of "world" to those things which we experience through the senses. According to Rahner what we call the world extends beyond that which is immediately observable and what we call our body does not "stop where our skin stops . . . in some sense we are an open system."[6]

In the all-cosmic dimension, the person becomes open to the universe and united to the basic unity of the world. Rahner says that there is in the world and in the universe a ground of unity in which all things communicate. Rahner speaks of the basic unity of the world as " . . . the basic oneness of the world, so difficult to grasp, yet so very real, by which all things in the world are related and communicate."[7] " . . . the soul, by surrendering her limited bodily structure in death becomes open towards the 'all.' "[8]

In order to understand what Rahner means by the "all" or the basic unity of the universe, it is necessary to understand what Rahner means by the *supernatural existential.* The supernatural existential may be understood as an existential or a demand of the natural world for the supernatural. Rahner speaks many times of the supernatural existential. He describes it as " . . . a burning longing for God . . . a capacity for God."[9]

For Rahner the creation of humankind, the world and the universe was a supernatural, not a natural event. Rahner rejects any theory that holds that first God created humankind and the world in a natural state and then gifted his creation with supernatural life or grace.[10] Creation has always been the gift of God sharing his very self.

For Rahner, creation and the incarnation of the word of God are two phases of the one act—God expressing himself in creation. The word of God became flesh and truly became a part of human reality. Christ has already transformed human history and the world. Rahner states that Christ has become the heart of the world.[11] Christ is the basic unity in which all creation is centered and interrelated. Christ, the word of God, has taken on the world and the universe. Christ exists forever in the state of *material incarnation.* The word of God, made visible to us as Jesus, and now risen as Christ, has become truly part of the world and the universe.[12]

In death, the person enters into a new relationship with

this world which has been transformed by Christ. Now this transformed world may be understood as the body by which the person now expresses himself or herself.

Although it it impossible to image how this body "looks," it is certainly not a physical body. Rahner says that in the all-cosmic dimension the person becomes united to the basic unity of the world. That is the unity of all things in which all things in the world and universe communicate. Rahner says that even before death persons are in communication with this core unity of the universe. Perhaps this helps to explain parapsychological events such as telepathy in which we experience our interrelatedness without understanding how or why.

In death the person becomes open to this unity and expresses himself or herself through the basic unity of the world. It is not only individually that persons become united with the basic oneness of the world but collectively. In Rahner's thought it is through the countless persons uniting themselves with the world and the universe that the cosmos is spiritualized. All of creation is becoming conscious of itself.[13]

If the world and the universe is becoming the body, in a certain sense, of persons who have died, the world is becoming the expression of these finite spirits. We are the world, and the sun, and the stars! We are finite spirit and we must express ourselves through material things. Therefore, in Rahner's understanding of the all-cosmic dimension of the soul, the soul, separated from the physical body in death, does not become removed from the world. Indeed, the soul expresses itself forever through the world and the universe.

We may ask ourselves: Is this at all possible? Is it possible that the whole material universe is somehow magnificently interrelated and that at death one enters into this cosmic interrelationship?

Surprisingly enough in today's world it is our scientists rather than our theologians we find first on their knees before the splendor of the material order—our world and the universe.

James Gleich, a science reporter for *The Times*, reports that while for the past thousand years science and faith have been enemies:

> Nowadays, we have incredible well-tuned constants of fundamental physics—to name just one, the gravitational force, which, if put ever-so-slightly out of whack, would have turned the universe into a collection of red dwarf stars or blue giant stars, either way presumably inhospitable to life.[14]

Something or someone is holding us all together. Rahner calls this interrelationship the all-cosmic dimension of the soul. In John Updikes' novel *Rogers Version*, the lead character, Dale Kohler says:

> The most miraculous thing is happening. . . . The physicists are getting down to the nitty-gritty, they've really just about pared things down to the ultimate details, and the last thing they ever expected to happen is happening. God is showing through.[15]

So death may not be the separation of the soul from the body. Death may be the opening up of the soul into an all-cosmic relationship that spans the sun, the stars, and the galaxies,

. . . the likes of which eye has not seen nor has ear heard

But whatever happened to particular and general judgment, heaven, hell, and purgatory?

NOTES

1. Rahner, "On the Intermediate State," *Theological Investigations* vol. 17, p. 121.
2. Rahner, *On the Theology of Death*, p. 34.

3. " . . . the teaching authority of the Church solemnly affirms that the Triune God is the Creator of the human creature, 'constituted,' as it were, alike of the spirit and the body (Lateran Council IV in 1215; Vatican Council I; Denz 3002) . . . that the rational or intellective soul is the form of the body in itself and essentially," Cf. "Human Soul," *New Catholic Encyclopedia*, vol. 13 (New York: Sheed & Ward), 1967, p. 462.

4. Rahner, *On the Theology of Death*, p. 31.

5. Ibid., p. 27.

6. Karl Rahner, "The Body in the Order of Salvation," *Theological Investigations*, vol. 17, p. 88.

7. Rahner, *On the Theology of Death*, p. 27.

8. Ibid, p. 31.

9. Rahner, *Theological Investigations*, vol. 1, trans. Cornelius Ernst, O.P. (Baltimore: Helicon Press, 1961), p. 312.

10. Thomas Knoebel, "Grace in the Theology of Karl Rahner: A Systematic Presentation" (unpublished dissertation: Fordham University, 1980), p. 32. It must be stressed, as Thomas Knoebel points out, that "Rahner explicitly rejects any two acts (historically or temporally) process on God's part whereby man is first created and then becomes a recipient of God's offered self-communication. There never is a 'time' when man exists as (pure) nature without the supernatural existential."

11. Karl Rahner, "A Spiritual Dialogue at Evening," *Theological Investigations*, vol. 3, trans. Karl Kruger (Baltimore: Helicon Press, 1967), p. 338.

12. Rahner, "The Festival of the Future of the World," *Theological Investigations*, vol.7, p. 183.

13. Rahner, *On the Theology of Death*, p. 73.

14. James Gleick, "Science on the Track of God," *The New York Times Magazine*, Jan. 4, 1987.

15. Ibid.

3

Purgatory, Hell and Judgment

We who live in the twentieth century have become so accustomed to directing our own lives that it is difficult for us to imagine that fullness of life is achieved in self-surrender. Karl Rahner tells us that that which makes our life valid and meaningful is the total surrender of self. The essence of our being is to tear ourselves away from ourselves in death to that incomprehensible mystery which we call God.[1] Rahner emphasizes that it is not only at the end of our lives that we give ourselves up but that throughout life we are called to surrender, trusting that the one who makes sense out of all reality is that other to whom we surrender.

It would seem that this total surrender of oneself in death is difficult enough so that life after death ought to be blissful and serene. However, the church teaches that immediately after death each person is judged and assigned to heaven, hell, or purgatory. Of these three, perhaps purgatory is the most perplexing.

Purgatory

The history of purgatory has undergone many developments and interpretations throughout the history of the church.[2]

In the early church, it appears that the idea of a purging place that existed between the death of an individual and his/her full entrance into heaven developed from the practice of praying for the dead. The early church thought of those who had died as falling into two groups: the apostles, martyrs, and prophets who entered heaven immediately at death, and ordinary Christians who were sinners. The church

... remembered that Our Lord and the Apostles had stated clearly that no one enters heaven unless he is sinless. The early Church did not seem to be very clear about where these souls were or how prayer could help them, but she definitely knew that prayer and sacrifice could be of benefit for those faithful Christians.[3]

The scriptural passage that is usually credited with referring to purgatory[4] is 1 Corinthians 3:11–15 in which Paul says:

And the quality of each person's work will be seen when the Day of Christ exposes it. For on that Day fire will reveal everyone's work, the fire will test it and show its real quality.

While there is much dispute over whether Paul was referring to a purging by fire which would occur before or after death, the practice of praying for the dead in order to relieve their suffering appears to have developed early in Christian practice.

In the Acts of St. Perpetua we read that she beheld her brother Dinocrates, who had died a heathen and was "suffering terrible torments, released from the place of punishment through her prayers."[5]

By the fourth century, St. Augustine gave a very exact description of purgatory. Augustine not only spoke of the importance of praying for the dead, but also described what was happening to them. Augustine wrote that those who had died but were not ready to enter heaven were purified by fire. Although Augustine did not describe the nature of this fire, there was no doubt that he believed that purgatory was a place of punishment.[6]

Early in the history of the church, disagreement developed over this understanding of purgatory. While many Christians agreed on the benefits of prayer for the dead, many others disagreed on the existence of purgatory as a place where persons were punished by fire.

In the year 1274, the church taught at the Council of Lyons that after death souls are cleansed by "purifying penalties" in purgatory and that the prayers of the living helped the dead.

By 1439, the church, at the Council of Florence, defined as doctrine, that is, a statement of belief held by Catholics, that souls are cleansed after death in purgatorial punishments and that the prayers of the living helped relieve the punishment of the dead.[7]

In the sixteenth century, Protestant groups who separated from the Roman Catholic Church rejected the idea of purgatory. In response to this, the church at the Council of Trent (1563) defined purgatory stating:

> The Catholic Church, by the teaching of the Holy Spirit, in accordance with the Sacred Scriptures and the ancient traditions of the Fathers, has taught in the holy councils, and most recently in this ecumenical council, that there is a purgatory and that the souls detained there are helped by the prayers of the faithful and especially by the acceptable Sacrifice of the Altar.[8]

While purgatory has been defined as part of the Catholic faith, two important points must be stressed: the idea of a fire that torments us and an understanding of a place where we spend time are not part of the church's definition.

What then is purgatory and how does Karl Rahner understand it?

Karl Rahner and Purgatory

It would seem that Karl Rahner struggled with the meaning of purgatory. At least, there appears to be a definite development in his understanding of purgatory over the years in his writings.

In 1966, Rahner spoke of purgatory as a "painful process."[9] At this time Rahner wrote that the process of purgatory could be "slower or quicker" depending on whether prayers were offered for the dead by the living.[10]

In 1970, Rahner wrote about purgatory as a period after death in which a person achieves full maturity. He said that purgatory was the state where the decision for God that the person had made in death permeated the whole person. At this point, Rahner held that purgatory was an "intermediate state," that is, a period between death and total fulfillment in heaven. He said,

> It cannot be denied that there is an intermediate state between death and bodily fulfillment . . . man reaches maturity in this intermediate state.[11]

In 1978, in *Foundations of the Christian Faith,* Rahner said, "We can hardly deny an interval in a person's destiny between death and the corporeal fulfillment of this person as a whole."[12]

But by 1981, in an article "On the Intermediate State," Rahner wrote that there was no intermediate state between death and heaven. He held that there was no interim period in which a soul after death existed while it waited for a glorified body. Rahner concluded that the idea of an intermediate state was a "stage in the history of theology and no more than that."[13]

Karl Rahner was not denying the existence of purgatory. He was in fact attempting to make it more compatible with the twentieth century person's understanding of what it means to be a human being and the relationship of human beings with the universe.

Rahner was constantly preoccupied by the modern person's struggle to believe in God. In our age, it is often difficult enough to believe in God when God's presence is frequently hidden from us. How is it possible to have faith in a God who demands total trust and self-surrender of us and then sentences us to a long period of painful punishment? Furthermore, the Catholic belief in indulgences or special dispensations which shorten the time spent in purgatory conveys the impression that purgatory is a place where one "does time," for a longer or shorter time depending on the arbitrary will of God.

Rahner felt that this kind of thinking about purgatory made the contemporary person uncomfortable. What happens, he asked, if two persons die and only one has an indulgence? Rahner says that this idea of remission of time spent in purgatory conveys the impression of a God or church which arbitrarily forgives some persons more quickly than others. Rahner says:

> If modern man hears of two people dying in a similar condition, and one is said to go straight to heaven because he happens to be the recipient of a papal indulgence, whereas the other spends many years in Purgatory, because the Pope, as the keeper of the keys of heaven, has not opened up straightaway; he will regard indulgences, represented in this way, as a clerical invention against which his own idea of God radically protests. It will not be easy to convince him that God desires the salvation of all men. . . .[14]

The idea of purgatory as a place where we go after death to be punished because we are not yet good enough to enter heaven and where some persons get out sooner than others because they have a special dispensation is not very appealing.

Rahner closely studied the images that are associated with purgatory. In considering the teachings of the church on life after death, it is important to remember that these teachings are conveyed in images. Each of us responds with a mental image when we hear the words purgatory, hell, or heaven. Rahner holds that while these images convey important truths which are part of our Catholic faith; he also points out that it is necessary to examine these images carefully in order to discover what is fact and what is myth.

In considering the idea of purgatory, Rahner holds that
there are many mythological aspects which have become part
of the contemporary image and which are not part of the
church's teaching. One of these mythological aspects which
Rahner rejects is the image of purgatory as a period of time.

Rahner believes that we are tyrannized by our concept of
time so that we envision life "after" death as a continuation of
acts and events in a linear fashion. Human beings tend to
imagine purgatory, hell, and heaven as being made up of endless days, weeks, months, and years. Rahner points out that
purgatory is not a place or state of being where we spend
time. He notes: "Eternity is not an infinitely long mode of
time but rather is a mode of spiritual freedom."[15]

Rahner reminds us that in death time ends completely.
There are no todays and tomorrows for those who have died.
In death we enter a state of being in which time no longer
exists. Death is beyond time. Time is only a temporary state
in which human beings are born, grow, and achieve fullness
and completion in death. Rahner points out that when we
understand time in this manner, then this understanding

> . . . imposes upon us an attitude of radical seriousness toward
> this life. Life is truly historical, that is, unique, irrepeatable of
> irrevocable significance. Life is suspended between a genuine
> beginning and a genuine end.[16]

Rahner also rejects the idea that we somehow get better in
purgatory in the sense that we are capable of changing our
decision for or against God. Rahner holds that the decision
made in death for or against God is final. There are no second
chances.

Rahner points out that by the free decision made in death,
a person decides once and for all his whole being.

> . . . man by his free decision *is* really so good or evil in the very
> ground of his being itself, that his final salvation or damnation
> are already given in this. . . . [17]

What then is purgatory?

Rahner notes that the idea of purgatory or an intermediate state between death and final perfection is not only found in the Catholic faith. He points out that the idea of reincarnation or a series of reincarnations which is held by many religions reveals the same human desire. The idea of purgatory, says Rahner, reveals something about the way human beings understand themselves. Purgatory reveals a dimension of human experience.[18]

Rahner insists that purgatory must be thought of not only as something that happens to us in death, but also as something that reveals who we are and what we long to become. All persons long for harmony and integration. We long to be one with ourselves, with others, and with the universe. Which one of us has looked at an endless vista of waves crashing on an ocean beach and not felt a sense of wonder at the rhythm and harmony of the universe? Which one of us has looked at the myriad stars which fill the sky and not felt a sense of longing to be one, to be whole, and to be in harmony with creation?

This longing for harmony and integration is part of our present human experience. Whether we are conscious of it or not, we long to integrate the many levels of our person into wholeness. We long to be one with those whom we love. Indeed, we long to reach out and become part of all creation.

Contemporary psychological insights have revealed that there are many levels or dimensions to the person. The modern person understands that he/she is multi-dimensional and that there are aspects of our personality which are sometimes hidden from our sight. We do not yet understand the role and relationship of our conscious, subconscious, and unconscious levels.

Rahner holds that each person longs to achieve not only an inner harmony, an integration of our true selves, but that we also long for an outer harmony with all of creation.

This full integration and harmonization of the individual, says Rahner, is what purgatory is.

Rahner's understanding of purgatory as a process of integration can best be understood in the light of his understanding of the all-cosmic relationship into which the person enters in death.

We have seen that Rahner understands that in death, the person gives up the limits of a particular physical body. However, because the soul needs an enduring relationship with matter, the person enters into an all-cosmic relationship with the material order, that is, the world and the universe.

When each person enters into relationship with the unity of the material order which has been assumed by Christ, the person experiences his/her own lack of integration and disharmony. The disharmony of his/her life is experienced as being in contradiction with his/her final perfected being.[19] Rahner says, "Now the painful process by which this contradiction is overcome is his purgatory."[20]

Purgatory is that integration by which a person achieves harmony with himself or herself, the world, and the universe which has been transformed by Christ.

Rahner's understanding of purgatory is compatible with the teaching of the church on the benefit of prayers for the dead.

In Rahner's understanding of the all-cosmic dimension of the person, death does not sever our relationship with those who are alive. The dead are not disembodied spirits who exist on another plane of existence. Rather, the living and the dead continue to be in relationship since they are both part of the material order of the world and the universe. Human beings are made up of body and soul, or, as Rahner says, spirit-matter. By the very essence of our being, we cannot be separated from matter or from spirit.

It is important to note that Rahner is not speaking from a scientific perspective but from the perspective of a person of faith who believes that the material order has been assumed by Christ. In today's world, a new global awareness, made possible only by the advent of the space age, has made humankind aware as never before of its interrelatedness as a global community. Human beings today must consider their destiny as members of a common sphere of being. We truly are "one of a piece." Our purpose is not to escape the world and the universe but to enter into an ever deeper relationship with the universe and the whole community of humankind. Jesus prayed:

> Father, may they all be one. May they be in us, just as you are in me and I am in you. May they all be one . . . (Jn 17:21).

Purgatory is that integration of ourselves, which we experience even now, into the reality of humankind, the world, and the cosmos being gathered up by Christ as a gift to the Father through the power of the Holy Spirit.

Rahner's understanding of purgatory is certainly more inviting than the image of a place where one is burned by fire for hundreds or a few thousand years. But then is hell a place where one suffers the eternal fires of damnation or is it not?

Hell

The traditional images of hell which have been conveyed to us are scenes of fire, devils, and howls of pain of the dammed. Since the time of ancient Christianity, various authors have attempted to propose an alternative to eternal damnation. There have been some who have suggested that at the end of time even those in hell will be forgiven and hell will cease to exist. Could a loving God allow an eternity of damnation?

At the same time, throughout the history of Christianity, a multitude of "fire and brimstone" preachers have put the fear of hell into their congregations with vivid descriptions of the tortures of the dammed.

Is there a hell? What does Rahner think hell is?

The church teaches that hell does indeed exist. Those who are condemned enter hell immediately at death and remain there for all eternity.[21]

Karl Rahner begins his reflection on hell by reminding us

again that it is important to look behind the symbols and
images of hell in order to discover what hell really reveals
about human experience.

Rahner says that our belief in hell reveals the real possibility
of a person to damn himself or herself. Hell is the real ability of
a person to become the antithesis of all that a person is meant
to be. Hell is becoming a non-person, a non-entity.[22]

In discussing what it means to be a person, Rahner states
that while each person is multi-dimensional, (that is our per-
sonalities are made up of many varied aspects), each person
is also essentially a unity. Each of us experiences that part of
our personality which we acknowledge as our "real self."
"You know or you do not know the *real* me," we frequently
say. Each of us desires that that which we experience as the
core of our person—the real me—will endure as eternally
valid.

According to Rahner's understanding we are never more
ourselves than in death. The whole life of a person is summed
up in the final and total decision made in death. In death, the
person achieves total fulfillment of who he or she is. For this
reason, Rahner says that a very important part of the church's
teaching on hell is that those who are damned enter hell immediately at death.[23]

Hell is that state of being which is the antithesis of what it
means to be human. Rahner holds that it is the essence of
human beings to reach out from themselves to the other. Human beings achieve self-knowledge by reaching out to others.
We discover who we are by our experience with others. We
discover our true selves by giving ourselves away.

We have also seen that Rahner holds that it is the very
essence of our nature as human beings to surrender ourselves
in death. Everything about us longs to say yes to that infinite
horizon which we call God. Hell, according to Rahner, is the
refusal to surrender oneself. Hell is a drive toward self-
centeredness and self-autonomy. This reversal of the drive
toward self-surrender sets the person in contradiction with
one's very self, with humankind, the cosmos, and God. Since

the ultimate decision of who we are is made in death, the refusal to surrender oneself in death results in the person being invalid and in contradiction with all that it means to be human for eternity.

Hell, cautions Rahner, ought not to be considered simply as a punishment which awaits us in the future; hell is experienced in the present.[24]

The drive toward self-centeredness and self-autonomy is a condition which pervades human society. It must be noted here that Rahner, in speaking of self-centeredness, is not discussing the affirmation of oneself. Any denial of self which damages or limits all that a person is meant to be is anti-human and therefore unholy.

Rahner is speaking of the drive toward self-autonomy as that drive which seeks to ignore or destroy our integral relationship with all of creation. This drive results in the destruction of our true selves, and alienation, an antagonism toward the created order.[25]

On an individual level, hell is experienced as an isolation from and antagonism toward ourselves, others, and God. Hell is when that isolation and antagonism become irrevocable. For creatures of whom scripture says, "It is not good for human beings to be alone," eternal isolation is the arch-contradiction of all that we are meant to be.

Furthermore, says Rahner, hell ought not to be considered as a condition which affects just the individual; hell is a condition which exists collectively in human society.[26]

In our age especially, our understanding of the interrelatedness of the whole cosmos radically affects our understanding of what hell is. We, in the twentieth century, are individuals who have entered the space age. From the very first time that our astronauts looked at the spinning blue planet earth from outer space, our perspective of who we are and what our place is in the universe has changed. It is easier for us to see that we are part of a common sphere of being. We are "one of a piece" with all creation. We are children of the universe called to realize our fullness and perfection in unity with all creation.

And yet, it is impossible to deny the existence of hellish conditions on a global scale. Hell is not a little red devil with a pitchfork stroking the fires of a far-off furnace. Hell is any condition where what is anti-human is created or allowed to exist. Hell is thousands of people dying of malnutrition or without homes; hell is hundreds of children jailed in South Africa; hell is any corrupt political, economic, or religious system which wantonly oppresses human beings.

Hell is industrial waste and abuse, toxic gas leaks and the capability of nuclear arms to obliterate this planet.

Karl Rahner notes that as Christians we are asked to believe only in the possibility, not the inevitability, of hell.[27] The thought is comforting. Perhaps no one will ever set himself or herself in contradiction with what it means to be human. Yet Rahner's understanding of hell is chilling.

Hell is the very real ability to negate ourselves as individuals, as societies, and even on a global scale. God said, "Let it be!" Free human beings have the power to say, "It shall not be."

Who decides then whether or not a person is condemned to hell? Who judges us?

The Particular Judgment

Popular imagery concerning the particular judgment usually has the newly dead person appearing at the gates of heaven. There he or she is confronted by St. Peter, keeper of the keys which open the gates. St. Peter interrogates the person on his or her behavior in life based on a detailed record which has apparently been kept in heaven. Understood in this way, the particular judgment seems to be a comprehensive examination on life.

The church teaches that there are two types of judgment. There is a particular judgment, which each individual experiences immediately at death, and there is a general judgment of all humankind at the end of the world.

The particular judgment of the individual has never been clearly defined by the church. However, in councils of the church (Council of Lyons 1274) and statements of the popes (*Benedictus Deus* of Pope Benedict XII in 1336) the teaching that persons who die are immediately assigned to heaven, hell, or purgatory implies that some kind of judgment takes place.[28]

Once again, Karl Rahner notes that the images which we associate with the idea of the particular and general judgment must be carefully studied. Rahner states that it is obvious that these images intend to say something very essential and very real.

Karl Rahner believes that at the moment of death each of us experiences a particular judgment.

However, there are two aspects of Rahner's understanding of the particular judgment that are striking.

First, Rahner understands the particular judgment not as a far-off examination of one's life which one submits to after death, but as an ever-present reality which pervades all life now.

Second, Rahner holds that there is no time interval between the particular judgment of an individual and the general judgment at the end of the world. Each of these needs further exploration.

In order to understand Rahner's insights into judgment, it is necessary to understand the person and mission of Christ as proclaimed in the gospel of John and its profound influence on Rahner.

In the beginning was the Word,
    and the Word was with God,
    and the Word was God.
He was in the beginning with God.
All things came to be through him,
    and without him nothing came to be (Jn 1:1–3).

And the Word became flesh
    and made his dwelling among us,

and we saw his glory,
the glory as of the Father's only Son,
full of grace and truth (Jn 1:14).

Rahner understands that because the word of God became flesh, God has already become the innermost life not only of each person but of all creation. According to Rahner, God is not merely a concept or a category. The presence of God in all human reality has already been accomplished by the word becoming flesh. God has already freely given himself in the incarnation of the word. The word of God visible in Jesus Christ has become in the risen Christ an intimate part of each of us, of human history, and of the final destiny of creation.[29]

The word of God has become part of creation so that it must be understood that the word is an ever present reality which pervades the whole of life. The word of God is the content and center of human existence such that the goal of all that human beings can be and the standard by which we judge ourselves is God himself.

For God did not send his Son into the world to condemn the world, but that the world might be saved through him. Whoever believes in him will not be condemned, but whoever does not believe has already been condemned because he has not believed in the name of the only Son of God. And this is the verdict, that the light came into the world, but people preferred darkness to the light, because their works were evil (Jn 3:17–19)

It has been shown that Rahner understands that it is the essence of being human to reach out to the other. That other, whom we long for and which is actually God, is already part of our present reality and the standard by which we judge ourselves. God has become the center of human reality, although now present in a hidden way. It is in the light of God's presence that we judge ourselves.

Rahner is saying that God is not some far-off deity in the

sky or apart from our life. God is the foundation of human life. It is God who is the horizon that human beings reach out to and in that reaching out experience knowledge of self, others, and creation. It is God who allows us to experience reality. God is present at every moment of our activity. We meet God everywhere in our quest to be all that we can be, says Rahner. God is indeed the judge of all our being, not in the sense of a judge who imposes a penalty on us but as the infinite horizon which is the goal of all that we can become. In this sense, we judge ourselves.

We set the standard for all that we become by reaching out or not reaching out to God who is the core of our being.

According to Rahner, in death the judgment which one has made throughout life is fixed for all eternity. In Rahner's thought, the particular judgment is not a sentence imposed on us by God, but rather is the fulfillment of all that the person has tried to become in life.

Rahner differentiates between the particular and general judgment by noting:

> It may be said that the particular or personal judgment is primarily concerned with the destiny of the individual insofar as he is not just an element in the collectivity of mankind. The general judgment speaks of the fact that mankind and its history, as a collective unity, comes under God's judgment.[30]

It is not surprising that Rahner points out the distinction between each individual's judgment and the collective judgment of humankind. While noting that each individual is necessarily part of the general judgment, each of us is individually responsible for the person we become. At the same time, every human being today must judge his/her participation in the world as a member of a collective history of humankind which extends backward and forward. Human history is "one of a piece." We are responsible for all that humankind and that creation becomes since we are inescapably a part of the whole. What is surprising is that Rahner holds that each per-

son's individual judgment and the general judgment of all
humankind occur simultaneously.

Rahner holds that all eschatological statements, that is,
statements about the last things such as the particular and
general judgment, " . . . are a transposition into the future of
something which a Christian person experiences in grace as
his present. . . ."[31]

Rahner says of the general judgment:

> (When) . . . we read that people will be gathered together by
> the angels and divided into two groups, the good and the evil,
> the sheep and the goats . . . it is obvious that these are images
> which intend to say something very essential and very real.
> But they intend to say just what can be said by Christian an-
> thropology about the last things, and nothing else.[32]

What Rahner means is that the images we associate with
the particular and general judgment do not tell us only about
the future. These images, says Rahner, also reveal what we
understand about present human experience. The particular
and general judgment reveal that God is already present in
the center of human existence as the standard by which we
judge ourselves. Rahner holds that the important truth conveyed by the idea of a particular and general judgment is the
interrelationship of the fate of the individual and the collective destiny of the world. These teachings reveal who we are
as humans, individual and collectively, in the present.

Rahner believes that if we interpret these teachings as de-
scribing events which are to take place in the far-off future, not
only are we likely to be unaffected by its meaning in our lives
now, but also we ignore the fact that human history has already been transformed by the incarnation of Christ. Rahner
says:

> Christ is already at the heart and center of all the poor things of
> the earth. . . . He is present in the history of the earth, whose
> blind course he steers with unearthly accuracy through all vic-

tories and all defeats to the day predestined for it, to the day on which his glory will break out of its own depths to transform all things.[33]

Therefore, according to Rahner, we must understand the particular and general judgment not as something that will happen to us only in the far-distant future but as an ever present reality which pervades the totality of life and in the light of which all creation is judged.

Because we believe in the incarnation of the word of God, we believe that all creation has already been transformed. Incarnation is an on-going event in which God gifts all creation with his presence. We believe also that the life, death, and resurrection of Jesus Christ are historical events which are permanent, definitive, and unchangeable. Salvation and redemption have already happened. The final judgment has been made. It is in the light of the fullness of Christ that all creation is judged.

However, it is also toward the manifestation of this fullness of Christ that all creation groans and strains. "He knows that all creation is groaning in labor pains even until now, and not only that, but we ourselves, who have the first fruits of the Spirit, we also groan within ourselves as we wait for adoption, the redemption of our bodies" (Rom 8:22–23).

In death, we who were created as free beings achieve the fullness of freedom of children of God. Rahner understands that there is no time interval between the particular judgment and the general judgment at the end of time. Death is beyond time. While we who are alive and confined by limits of space and time look forward to the future in which the final judgment will be made manifest, those who have died exist in a state of being which is eternal. In this state of being, weeks, months, and years no longer chip away at and erode our existence. Existence consists of the eternal "now." In this fully achieved existence, individuals are fully aware that self-identity is achieved through union with the whole of creation transformed by Christ. The particular judgment of the individual is intimately and indelibly a part of the final destiny of all creation. We will achieve at last that for which we were created.

"Behold, God's dwelling is with the human race! He will dwell with them, and they will be his people and God himself will always be with them . . . " (Rev 21:3).

But then is there no second coming of Christ and the end of the world in space and time?

NOTES

1. Karl Rahner, *Theological Investigations*, Vol. XIII. Translated by David Bourke (London: Darton, Longman and Todd, 1975), p. 182.

2. Cf. Jacques Le Goff, *La Naissance Du Purgatoire* (Paris: Gallinard, 1981).

3. E.J. Fortman, S.J., *Everlasting Life after Death* (New York: Alba House, 1976), p. 110.

4. Ibid., p. 128.

5. Ibid., p. 129.

6. Ibid., p. 130.

7. J. Neuner, S.J. and J. Dupuis, S.J., *The Christian Faith*, p. 18.

8. E.J. Fortman, S.J., *Everlasting Life after Death*, p. 132.

9. Karl Rahner, "A Brief Study of Indulgences," *Theological Investigations*, Vol. X, translated by David Bourke (London: Darton, Longman and Todd, 1973), p. 165.

10. Ibid., p. 164.

11. Karl Rahner, "Theological Observations on the Concept of Time," *Theological Investigations*, Vol. XVII, translated by Margaret Kohl (London: Darton, Longman, and Todd, 1981) p. 303.

12. Karl Rahner, *The Foundations of the Christian Faith*, translated by William V. Dych (New York: Seabury Press, 1978), p. 442.

13. Karl Rahner, "On the Intermediate State," *Theological Investigations*, Vol. 17, p. 118.

14. Gerald A. McCool, ed., *A Rahner Reader* (New York: The Seabury Press, 1979), p.73.

15. Karl Rahner, *The Foundations of the Christian Faith*, p. 437.

16. Karl Rahner, *On the Theology of Death*, translated by Charles H. Henkey (New York: Herder and Herder, 1971), p. 35–36.

17. Ibid., p. 61.

18. Karl Rahner, *The Foundations of the Christian Faith*, p. 442.

19. Karl Rahner "A Brief Study on Indulgences," *Theological Investigations*, Vol. X, p. 303.

20. Ibid., p. 165.

21. E.J. Fortman, *Everlasting Life After Death*, p. 161.

22. Karl Rahner, *On the Theology of Death*, p. 60.

23. Karl Rahner, ed., "Hell," *Sacramentum Mundi: An Encyclopedia of Theology* (New York: Seabury Press, 1968–1970), Vol. 3, p. 7.

24. Ibid., p. 8.

25. Gerald McCool, ed., "On Christian Dying," *A Rahner Reader*, p. 355.

26. Karl Rahner, *On the Theology of Death*, p. 61

27. Karl Rahner, "Eschatology," *Sacramentum Mundi*, Vol. 2, p. 245.

28. J. Neumer, S.J. and J. Dupuis, S.J., *The Christian Faith*, p. 18.

29. Karl Rahner, "The Hermeneutics of Eschatological Assertions," *Theological Investigations*, Vol. IV, translated by Kevin Symth (Baltimore: Helicon Press, 1967), p. 39.

30. Karl Rahner, "Particular Judgment," *Sacramentum Mundi*, Vol. 3, p. 275.

31. Karl Rahner, *The Foundation of the Christian Faith*, p. 433.

32. Ibid.

33. Karl Rahner, "Hidden Victory." *Theological Investigations*, Vol. VII, p. 157.

4

The Second Coming of Christ

All of us long for a future worth hoping for. We long to see our dreams and plans fulfilled in a future which offers us peace, love, and joy. Karl Rahner says that the image of the second coming of Christ reveals that there really is a future worth hoping for. Today, more than ever, persons are concerned about the future and destiny of the world and of all humankind. We want to know what the future will be like. We often wonder if there will be a future.

Rahner holds that the image of the second coming of Christ gives us hope that there is meaning not only for our individual lives but also for all of human life. When we pray, "Christ has died, Christ is risen, Christ will come again," we are stating our conviction that the goal of human life is the manifestation of Christ in all his glory. Despite the vicissitudes of our lives, there is a method to the madness. There is meaning not only to our lives but also to our death and dying.

Our hope for the future is that Christ has really become a part of the whole material order, the world and the universe. The reality of Christ has been grafted into the world and the universe so that Christ has not only become a part of all human life and its history, but he has also become the destiny of the world.

Because Christ is present now in human lives and history,

the world as a whole and each personal life is already different than what it might have been if Christ had not taken it on as his own.[1]

But, cautions Rahner, we must not think that the image of the second coming of Christ gives us hope only for the future; it also helps us to better understand our present experience. The image of the second coming of Christ reveals that the future we hope for is present now. Rahner says that the image of the second coming of Christ reveals "the unfathomable depth and richness of our present existence, of that existence which often gives the impression of nothing but banalities."[2]

All of human reality and human history has been taken on as his own by Jesus Christ and has been transformed by him. Rahner says that we must understand the image of the second coming of Christ as revealing that the glory and fulfillment toward which humankind is heading as its final destiny is already present. Christ is risen as he said and is indeed present in our lives! Rahner says,

> Christ is already at the heart and center of all the poor things of the earth. . . . He is present in the history of the earth, whose blind course he steers with unearthly accuracy through all victories and all defeats to the day predestined for it, to the day on which His glory will break out of its own depths to transform all things.[3]

Christ is already present in our lives and in our history both as individuals and as part of all humankind. Christ has taken on the history of all humankind as his own. By his death and resurrection, Christ has become a permanent part of the human reality. When we ask ourselves whether or not our life has meaning, we are able to answer that life is indeed meaningful because Jesus Christ has become part of it—part of each individual's life and part of the life of all humankind.

In order to understand Rahner's position that all of the human reality and its history has been transformed by Christ, it is necessary to consider Rahner's understanding of the rela-

tionship of the historical Jesus of Nazareth and the risen
Christ.

In the world today, one may well ask who is this Jesus of
Nazareth and what does this man who lived so long ago have
to do with my life? It might be said that our contemporary
society experiences the lack of meaning of life and the loss of
hope for the future as no other age has. In our world today
widespread materialism, Freudian pyschological interpretations of life after death as an illusion we create to deny fear of
our own extinction, philosophical interpretations that life is
absurd, and the ever present threat of global nuclear annihilation lead the modern person to question the meaning not only
of his/her own existence but also the meaning of all life.

And yet we dare to pray, "Christ has died, Christ is risen,
Christ will come again," and to say that this statement gives
meaning not only to our own lives but to the destiny of all
creation.

When Rahner asks the question "Who is Jesus and what is
his relationship to the risen Christ?" he notes first that all our
statements of belief about Jesus refer to a quite definite historical person and to historical events.[4]

There really was a Jesus of Nazareth born into time and
space. However, when Rahner discusses the relationship of
the historical Jesus who laughed and wept, ate and drank,
and the risen Christ, Rahner centers his discussion on the
words "And the word became flesh" (Jn 1:14). Jesus of Nazareth is the word of God become flesh!

In Rahner's understanding, creation and the incarnation of
the word are two aspects of the one act of God. God wished to
express himself and communicate himself. God's communication was the incarnation of the word in all creation. In this
act, God gave himself away in absolute self-communication to
that which was totally different than himself, that is, creation
of the material order.

The word of God, the second person of the Blessed Trinity,
took on the human nature of Jesus of Nazareth. God truly
became one of us. Jesus was the means by which the word of

God expressed himself. It was through the real flesh and blood of Jesus of Nazareth that God was made visible to us.

> And the Word became flesh
> and made his dwelling among us,
> and we saw his glory:
> the glory as of the Father's only Son,
> full of grace and truth (Jn 1:14).

Rahner holds that the union of the word of God and the historical Jesus was not only a unique experience—God did not become man in any other—it was also a real union. Rahner says, "One must not think of the God-man as if God or his Logos (Word of God) had put on a kind of livery for the purpose of his saving treatment of man, or as if he had disguised himself, as it were, and had given himself merely an external appearance to enable him to show himself in the world."[5]

The Word of God truly took on the human nature of Jesus. At the same time, Jesus was truly human. Rahner says: "Jesus is true man; he is truly part of the earth, truly a moment of human natural history, for he is born of woman. . . ."[6]

There are facts we know about the historical Jesus, about his teaching, his deeds, his awareness of his mission that occurred in a specific time and place. He was a man like us in all things except sin, and yet when we read the gospel accounts of him, we wonder what was in that voice or what light shone in those eyes so that those who heard his request "Follow me" left all they called their own. What kind of man was this that crowds flew to his side and, as the gospel says, he healed the wounded bodies and those who were wounded inside? What kind of man is this who still is spoken of two thousand years after his life and death?

When we read the gospels to discover who Jesus is, we are aware that these testaments of the life and death of Jesus were written years after his death and resurrection. We understand that they were written from the perspective of persons who had powerfully experienced the resurrection and knew that Christ was alive! This awareness colored their interpretation of the sayings and deeds of Jesus of Nazareth.

We may ask ourselves how this historical Jesus of Nazareth became the Christ of faith, the Christ that we profess will come again.

In order to understand the Christ who will come again, it is necessary to consider Rahner's understanding of the death and resurrection of Jesus.

Rahner notes that the death of Jesus of Nazareth was essentially similar to all deaths. At the same time, Jesus' death was radically different than any other death.

In our study of Rahner's understanding of death, we have seen that for Rahner death is that act in which we are most fully ourselves. Since human beings are made of finite spirit and matter, in death the person achieves the essence of his/her being—that is, self-surrender to absolute mystery. While it is the essence of finite spirit to surrender itself to the incomprehensible mystery which we call God, it is also of the essence of finite spirit to maintain an enduring relationship with matter. While human beings are within the limits of time and space, our physical bodies are the means by which finite spirit expresses itself. At death, finite spirit breaks free of the limits of space and time and expresses itself in an all-cosmic relationship with the material order of the world and the universe.[7]

According to Rahner, Jesus of Nazareth experienced death as humans do. He totally surrendered himself to that incomprehensible mystery whom he called "Father." "Father, into your hands, I commend my spirit" (Lk 23:46).

In and through his death, Jesus brought to completion his human existence in time and space and fully expressed all that he was in the act of surrender to his Father.

But Jesus' death is also radically different than ours. Jesus' death is, as it is for us, the fullest expression of all that we are. But Jesus' death is the fullest expression of the human nature of Jesus of Nazareth which was assumed by the word of God.[8]

Our Christian faith tells us that which we would not dare to surmise on our own. God so loved the world that he gave us the gift of himself. God communicated himself to us through the incarnation of the word of God. The word of God, the second person of the Blessed Trinity, took on the human nature of Jesus and expressed itself through the flesh of Jesus. It was through the real flesh and blood of Jesus that God became visible to us. The word of God truly became flesh. God communicated himself to us by becoming one of us. The word of God became part of the human reality and the material order, the world and the universe. By assuming the human nature of Jesus, the word of God became part of the whole human reality of Jesus of Nazareth, his life, his death, and his resurrection.

Just as for us death is the fullest expression of all that we are, so too the death of Jesus was the fullest expression of the human nature of Jesus which had been assumed by the infinite word of God. In Jesus' death, the reality of Jesus Christ opened up into the basic oneness of the world and entered into a permanent relationship with all of the material order. Within the limits of time and space, the word of God expressed itself through the physical body of Jesus of Nazareth. Through the death of Jesus, the word of God entered into an all-cosmic relationship with the material order which is expressed through the risen Jesus Christ.[9] The transformed material order is the means by which the resurrected Jesus Christ now expresses himself. Jesus Christ shows us that the meaning of human existence is best expressed in resurrection. Rahner says that Jesus Christ has made manifest that resurrection is the ultimate form of human existence.[10] Resurrection is our hope for the future.

Jesus Christ is truly risen. The Christ who is Jesus of Nazareth united with the word of God now expresses himself permanently through all creation. The perfection of humankind has already achieved total fulfillment in the risen Christ. The salvation of the total human reality has already been given to us in Jesus Christ. By his resurrection, Christ has revealed the ultimate form of human reality. Jesus Christ has made real all that human beings are meant to be.[11] Our final destiny is resurrection.

Our hope for the future is that we, too, shall rise from the dead. Human perfection and fulfillment means resurrection of the body. But resurrection is not a return to life in space and time. While it is impossible to imagine how this risen body "looks," Rahner holds that the risen body is the way we will express ourselves in the relationship we open out into with the material order at death.

Rahner further points out that each person can take part in a resurrection mode of being even now while still within the limits of space and time. Because of Christ's resurrection, he says, the world has already acquired a new heavenly dimension.[12] Because of the risen Christ, human history has now become part of a destiny which absolutely transcends human history. Our destiny is now the destiny of Jesus Christ. We have become part of the history of Jesus Christ, Son of Mary and Son of God. We have become part of God's own history![13]

Although Christ has taken on human history, human beings are still free and responsible for the development of temporal history. Human beings are responsible for that future which we can direct and fashion. We are responsible for what the world becomes.

Rahner emphasizes that we can never think of our individual destiny apart from the final destiny of all creation and therefore part of its final transformation. Since we are part of a common sphere of being, our individual choices and acts affect not only ourselves but the whole of reality. "We are one of a piece" with all humankind, the earth, and the stars!

Rahner's understanding of the second coming of Christ and the final transformation of the world emphasizes the individual's responsibility not only for his/her own personal development but for the development of the future of the world. All of us say, "I want to be all that I can be." What we become affects what the world becomes. In the same way, what the world becomes affects what we can become. The final transformation of the world is our own transformation.

Rahner points out that human beings have been given "a task with which we have been commissioned to fashion it (the future) and so to complete, in a process of historical evolution, the creative work of God himself."[14]

Because Christ has assumed our human reality, we have become co-creators with him. Together with Christ we are fashioning the future. We have become responsible for fashioning our own history. Not only do we have the right but we have the responsibility to shape our own future.

Each one of us sees the world through his/her own eyes, but because we are one of a piece, that is, interrelated and united with each other and all of creation, when we take responsibility for fashioning our own future, we fashion the future of the world in a very real way. The world is an expression of who we are, not a thing which is distinct from us. Because who we are influences and fashions the world, we must understand the expectations, the longings and the signs of the times of our world.

It would be a facile response to wonder why we should bother examining the signs of the times in our world today since all the signs are bad. While it is true that sin is an ever present reality and individual and global evidences of sin are often overwhelming, at the same time the reign of God is present among us. The image of the second coming of Christ teaches us that the world has indeed been transformed in Christ. Christ is present in our personal lives, in our joys and sorrows, our moments of despair and our instances of hope. When we examine our lives, we discover the loving presence of Jesus Christ with us. Our task is to discover this presence by examining our real lives and our present experience.

From time to time there are some who question this. Why spend time, they will say, reflecting on our day to day lives, personal relationships, community involvement, or hopes for the future, since the future is out of our hands? When we look at the life of Jesus, we discover that Jesus himself taught by reflecting on his day to day experience. It was Jesus who taught us to "look at the lilies of the field." Jesus told stories that reverberated with human experience so that two thousand years later men and women still hear their story being told in the tale of the prodigal son or the woman who searched for the lost coin.

Christ is present in our daily lives. "The whole created world eagerly awaits the revelation of the children of God" (Rom 8:19).

However, we must also remember that we cannot carry on this reflection on life alone. We are together on this journey with the rest of humankind. We need to communicate with each other. It is ironic that in a nation in which none of us ever seems to stop talking, the most often cited interpersonal problem is "lack of communication." Husbands and wives, parents and children, friends and associates will frequently state that they do not or cannot understand each other or make themselves understood.

We are called to be a dialogic people, but dialogue is no easy task. Speaking one's truth and listening with the heart demands courage and perseverance. It is not a task, however, which can be dismissed. It is through dialogue that we build community. It is through dialogue that we become aware of the presence of Christ in our lives. Only by sharing the gift of oneself and receiving the communication of life from the other can we truly enter into each other's experience and become one in mind and heart. This call to dialogue is a mandate from Jesus. Jesus prayed,

> I pray that they may all be one. Father, may they be in us, just as you are in me and I am in you (Jn 17:21).

Dialogue demands that we lay aside our customary mind-sets in order to be truly open to the other.

In a society which challenges Christian values, the commitment to speak one's truth unswervingly demands courage. In a society which glorifies self-gratification, the ability to reach out and receive the other demands self-sacrifice.

For years, perhaps consciously or unconsciously, there

have been many who in living out their Christian commitment have known that there is more to reality than that which meets the eye. They have looked at life and known that it was already transformed. They have shared and received with their hearts. They have always known that they were part of a story that was larger than the pages of their lives, and they have committed themselves to making this a better world.

In today's world, we are conscious of our interrelationship as no other age has ever been. But while one would hope that this awareness of global interrelatedness would mark a turning point in the contemporary attitudes of humankind, all of us know only too well that thousands of people are dying of malnutrition, hundreds of persons are jailed unjustly, terrorists hold the world at gunpoint, and corrupt political, economic, and religious systems wantonly oppress persons. Never before has humankind been so conscious of the deeply reciprocal nature of its union with each other and with the earth. At the same time humankind has developed the ability to obliterate this world with the push of a button.

In the world today, medical, scientific, and chemical advances offer us hope for the future that were only dreams in the past. Diseases which were once dreaded have become forgotten names and future cures are now real possibilities. But at the same time, industrial waste and abuse has allowed toxic gas leaks in distant places and in places perhaps as near as our own backyard to send shivers of fear up our spines. Recently new diseases have emerged which our technology appears powerless to deal with.

It is in the midst of these opposing forces and the rapidity of change which is characteristic of our times that we must question ourselves how the good news that the world has already been transformed by Christ can be proclaimed. How can we say to a world such as this: "Christ has died, Christ is risen, Christ will come again"?

How do we proclaim the gospel message to live simply in a society that says that things should always get bigger and better? How do we proclaim Jesus' message that we should love so much that we will lay down our lives for each other in a society that says we should emerge victorious out of every situation?

Is it possible to give witness to and invite others to a resurrection life-style in a society that makes materialism, practical and profitable results, a top priority in all areas of life?

Rahner says that the task of Christians today is to give contemporary society hope. We have hope for a future as described by St. Paul:

What eye has not seen, and ear has not heard,
and what has not entered the human heart,
what God has prepared for those who love him (1 Cor 2:9).

While human beings are responsible for that future which they can plan and direct, the "absolute future" cannot be planned or manipulated by humankind. The "absolute future" of all humankind and creation is given to us as a gift. That absolute future, which is our final destiny, is, according to Rahner, God/himself.

But the absolute future is even now part of our present reality. Rahner states that since we believe that the word of God has indeed become one of us, and that the death and resurrection of Christ are indeed historical events, God has entered our history in such a way that it has already been transformed. We already see that the perfect fulfillment of the history of humankind is finite spirit which is united with the material order in Christ!

Rahner says that at the end of time there will indeed be a new heaven and a new earth in which we will exist forever in a risen mode of being. Rahner believes that a transformed universe will be the culmination of a process in which spirit and matter have been involved since the dawn of creation,[15] when God so loved the world that the word became flesh and made his dwelling among us (Jn 1:14).

The book of Revelation describes the second coming of

Christ amidst trumpet blares and cataclysmic natural events that usher in a new heaven and a new earth.

> Then I saw a new heaven and a new earth. The former heaven and the former earth had passed away, and the sea was no more. And I also saw the holy city, a new Jerusalem, coming down out of heaven from God, prepared as a bride adorned for her husband. I heard a loud voice from the throne, saying "Behold, God's dwelling is with the human race. He will dwell with them and they will be his people and God himself will always be with them [as their God]. He will wipe away every tear from their eyes, and there shall be no more death or mourning, wailing or pain, [for] the old order has passed away."
>
> The one who sat on the throne said, "Behold, I make all things new." Then he said, "Write these words down, for they are trustworthy and true." He said to me, "They are accomplished. I [am] the Alpha and the Omega, the beginning and the end" (Rev 21:1–6).

Rahner says:

> The end of the world is, therefore, the perfection and total achievement of saving history which had already come into full operation and gained its decisive victory in Jesus Christ and his resurrection. In this sense his coming takes place at this consummation in power and glory: his victory made manifest, the breaking through into experience, and the becoming manifest for experience, too, of the fact that the world as a whole flows into his resurrection and into the transfiguration of his body. His Second Coming is not an event which is enacted in a localized manner on the stage of an *un*changed world which occupies a determined point in space in this world of our experience (how could everyone see it otherwise, for instance?); his Second Coming takes place at the moment of the perfecting of the world into the reality which he already possesses now, in such a way that he, the Godman, will be revealed to all reality and, within it, to every one of its parts in its own way, as the innermost secret and center of all the world and of all history.[16]

According to the fourth gospel:

He was in the world,
and the world came to be through him,
but the world did not know him.
He came to what was his own,
but his own people did not accept him.
But to those who did accept him
he gave power to become children of God (Jn 1:10–12).

It is easy now to see that we are on a journey, a journey of all creation. It is frightening and ennobling now to realize the extent of our power. It is urgent now to assume our responsibility. We are the world. We are the children. We are the children of the universe. We are creation which has been transformed by Jesus Christ. We are the children of God.

Jesus' final message to his apostles was:

"All power in heaven and on earth has been given to me.
Go, therefore, and make disciples of all nations,
baptizing them in the name
   of the Father,
   and of the Son,
   and of the holy Spirit,
teaching them to observe all that I have commanded you.
And behold I am with you always
   until the end of the age" (Mt 28:18–20).

But what about the church? Does the church in the world today agree with these things? Does the church agree with Karl Rahner?

NOTES

1. Karl Rahner, "Dogmatic Questions on Easter," *Theological Investigations*, trans. Kevin Smyth (Baltimore: Helicon Press, 1966), p. 129.

2. Karl Rahner, "Eternity from Time," *Practice of Faith: A Handbook of Contemporary Spirituality* (New York: Crossroad, 1983), p. 311.

3. Karl Rahner, "Hidden Victory," *Theological Investigations*, Vol. 7, trans. David Bourke (New York: Seabury Press, 1974), p. 157.

4. Gerald A. McCool, ed. "A Short Formula of Christian Faith" by Karl Rahner, *A Rahner Reader* (New York: Seabury Press, 1975, p. 209.

5. Ibid., "Christology Within an Evolutionary View of the World" by Karl Rahner, p. 169.

6. Ibid.

7. Karl Rahner, *On the Theology of Death*, trans. Charles H. Henkey (New York: Herder and Herder Press, 1965), passim.

8. Gerald A. McCool, ed. (op. cit.), "Christology Within an Evolutionary View of the World," pp. 167–169.

9. Karl Rahner, *On the Theology of Death*, pp. 71ff.

10. Karl Rahner, "On the Intermediate State," *Theological Investigations*, Vol. 17, trans. Margaret Kohl (London: Darton, Longman, and Todd, 1981), p. 121.

11. Karl Rahner, "Jesus' Resurrection," *Theological Investigations*, Vol. 17, p. 19.

12. Ibid.

13. Karl Rahner, "Some Implications of the Scholastic Concept of Uncreated Grace," *Theological Investigations*, Vol. 1, trans. Cornelius Ernst, O.P. (Baltimore: Helicon Press, 1963), p. 319.

14. Karl Rahner, "The Theological Problems Entailed in the Idea of the New Earth," *Theological Investigations*, Vol. 10, trans. David Bourke (London: Darton, Longman and Todd, 1973), p. 266.

15. Denis Burkhard et al., eds., "Man as Spirit and Matter," by Karl Rahner, *Man Before God* (New York: P.F. Kennedy & Sons, 1966), p. 26.

16. Gerald A. McCool, op. cit. "The Resurrection of the Body," p. 361.

5

A Comparison of Rahner's Eschatology with the Teaching of the Church

O Lord, our Lord,
  how glorious is your name over all the earth!
  You have exalted your majesty above the heavens.
Out of the mouths of babes and sucklings you have fashioned
    praises because of your foes.
to silence the hostile and the vengeful.
When I behold your heavens, the work of your fingers,
the moon and the stars which you set in place—
What is man that you should be mindful of him,
or the son of man that you should care for him?
You have made him little less than the angels,
  and crowned him with glory and honor.
You have given him rule over the works of your hands,
  putting all things under his feet:
  all sheep and oxen,
  yes and the beasts of the field,
The birds of the air, the fishes of the sea,
  and whatever swims the paths of the seas.
O Lord, our Lord,
  how glorious is your name over all the earth!

PSALM 8

What does the church say about death and the last things and how does it compare with Rahner's presentation of his eschatology?

Since Rahner's eschatology was influenced by his understanding of the essence of human beings, we will begin our study by examining the teaching of the church on the nature of human beings and comparing it to Rahner's thought.

"What is man that you should be mindful of him?" (Ps 8:4). The church teaches that although human beings are made up of body and soul, human beings are *substantially one* in being and in final destiny. Human beings are created by God, in body and soul, as the crown of creation (Fourth Lateran Council, 1215). Human souls do not exist in a previous existence outside of the body (Council of Constantinople, 1543). The soul is the form of the body. The soul is that which gives life to the body (Fourth Lateran Council, 1215).[1]

We have seen that Rahner understood human beings as made up of spirit and matter. According to Rahner's understanding of human beings, the human person is irrevocably anchored in matter by our very nature. Rahner notes that he prefers to speak of human beings made up of spirit and matter rather than body and soul since he says that the image of man as made up of body and soul

> only conveys man's essential being in a highly primitive way, because man is not really built up out of body and soul, but out of spirit and *materia prima* or first matter.[2]

William Thompson, in discussing Rahner's eschatology, points out that Rahner holds that in the traditional understanding of the nature of man the emphasis on man as made up of body and soul led to an individualism that the modern person finds incompatible with his/her understanding of his/her role in and relationship with the world today. The emphasis on man as made up of body and soul often leads to a dualistic image of the person which disparages our intimate and enduring relationship with the material world. This im-

age, furthermore, has had negative implications, with this
result:

> The earth and our linkage with it through the body and social
> responsibility are replaced in the Christian imagination by a
> fascination for eternity and our linkage with it through "soul."
> But for our contemporaries that eschatology becomes an other-
> worldly utopia and opiate for the people, fostering a kind of
> indifference to the misery of this world.[3]

In Rahner's thought, human beings are intimately linked
with the world. In time and space, the physical body is our
concrete expression of our spirit. Finite human spirit must
always express itself through matter. According to Rahner,
even within the present limits of time and space, human beings are entering into a relationship with all of the material
order, the world and the universe which has been transformed by Christ.

In the present time, the church teaches through the Second
Vatican Council that human beings are creatures who must
exist in relationships to matter. The council fathers say:

> . . . though made up of body and soul, man is one. Through his
> bodily composition he gathers to himself the elements of the
> material world. Thus they reach their crown through him and
> through him raise their voice in free praise of the Creator.[4]

In today's world, the council fathers point out that human
beings are becoming increasingly aware of their relationship
with the whole of human reality.

> The destiny of the human community has become all of a
> piece, where once the various groups of men had a kind of
> private history of their own. Thus, the human race has passed
> from a rather static concept of reality to a more dynamic, evolu-
> tionary one. In consequence, there has arisen a new series of
> problems, a series as important as can be, calling for new ef-
> forts of analysis and synthesis.[5]

Human beings today seek to understand who they are in the face of social, political and economic changes which are occurring on a global scale. The council fathers point out:

> Though mankind today is struck with wonder at its own discoveries and its power, it often raises anxious questions about the current trend of the world, about the place and role of man in the universe, about the meaning of his individual and collective strivings and about the ultimate destiny of reality and humanity.[6]

According to the teachings of the church, when we begin to examine the question of who human beings are, we must take into account the contemporary person's understanding of himself/herself as a being in relationship with the global human community.

We may say that Rahner's understanding of the nature of human beings not only is compatible with the teachings of the church but also reverberates with the contemporary person's experience. Rahner has expressed the contemporary person's experience as a being in relationship with all of humankind and the world. Despite the use of different terms, Rahner's understanding of the person is in accord with the teachings of the church. We are one spirit/matter (in body and in soul), and in union with all creation.

Rahner also understood that it is the essence of the human person to reach out toward incomprehensible mystery. The human person has an enduring relationship with the material order, but at the same time person as spirit is always reaching out toward otherness.

The council fathers of the Second Vatican Council point out that man

> . . . bears in himself an external seed which cannot be reduced to sheer matter.[7]

Rahner says that all human beings experience themselves as more than just their physical bodies. Human beings experience themselves as a longing for that which is more than themselves. Rahner points out that that which we long for is the absolute future to which humankind is destined. It is the essence of human nature to long for that absolute future which, consciously understood or not, is another name for God.

It is the nature of human beings to be directed toward the future. Rahner says that today humankind is experiencing a new understanding of our role in directing the future. He says that the world

> . . . has reached a second stage in realizing its potential: man himself takes it upon himself as a task with which he has been commissioned to fashion it (the future) and so to complete, in a process of historical evolution, the creative work of God himself.[8]

However, the awareness humankind has in this century of the power at our disposal to direct and plan our future has revealed problems never before encountered. The council fathers point out:

> Never has the human race enjoyed such an abundance of wealth, resources and economic power. Yet a huge proportion of the world's citizens is still tormented by hunger and poverty, while countless numbers suffer from total illiteracy. Never before today has man been so keenly aware of freedom, yet at the same time new forms of psychological slavery make their appearance. Although the world today has a very vivid sense of its unity and of how one man depends on another in needful solidarity, it is most grievously torn into opposing camps by conflicting forces.[9]

> As a result, buffeted between hope and anxiety and pressing one another with questions about the present course of events, they are burdened down with uneasiness. This same course of events leads men to look for answers. Indeed, it forces them to do so.[10]

In a similar manner, the American bishops in their pastoral letter on war and peace, *The Challenge of Peace: God's Promise and Our Response*, point out:

> We live today, therefore, in the midst of a cosmic drama; we possess a power which should never be used, but which might be used if we do not reverse our direction. We live with nuclear weapons knowing that we cannot afford to make one serious mistake. This fact dramatizes the precariousness of our position, politically, morally and spiritually.[11]

In such a world, Rahner notes that Christians today "must impress the framework of secular life with the stamp of their eschatological hope."[12] At the same time Rahner cautions against the temptation either to think of the future as being only that which man is capable of bringing about by his own manipulation or plans,[13] or to think of the ultimate future which awaits man as being so "other worldly" that man has no need or responsibility to tend to the reality of this world. Rahner points out that that future which Christians proclaim is the absolute future. This future is given to us as gift. This absolute future which is of the essence of man's nature to long for must be understood as part of our actual and present reality, although it is present in a hidden way. The future, then, must be understood as part of the present self-understanding of humankind.

According to Rahner's understanding, human beings must understand themselves and their present in its relationship to the absolute future. As we understand ourselves and our present, we understand that God who is the absolute future is always present in the center of human existence. Rahner says that the whole point of Christianity is that God is the center of human existence and actually wants to be so.[14] The whole point of our life is understanding that God has become part of it.

We see both in Rahner's thought and in the contemporary teaching of the church that there is a dramatic transformation taking place in our understanding of the person and his/

her responsibility for shaping the future. The contemporary
teaching of the church reveals a shift in the attitude of the
church from a static image of the human being to a more
dynamic understanding of the person as co-responsible with
God for fashioning the future. At the same time, the church
teaches the transcendence or absolute otherness of God and
cod's power in our lives. This teaching is in accord with
Rahner's understanding of the human being as responsible
for fashioning the future and yet gifted with an absolute future beyond our wildest dreams.

> What is man that you should be mindful of him. . . .
> You have made him little less than the angels and crowned him
>   with glory and honor.
> You have given him rule over the works of your hands,
> putting all things under his feet.

Death

The church teaches that death is a punishment for sin. In the
Council of Trent (1546), the church teaches that because of the
original sin committed by Adam and Eve, not only death and
suffering were transmitted to all his posterity but also the
guilt of sin. The documents of the Council of Trent (1546) say:

> If anyone asserts that Adam's sin harmed only him and not his
> descendants and that the holiness and justice received from
> God which he lost was lost only for him and not for us also; or
> that, stained by the sin of disobedience, he transmitted to all
> mankind only death and suffering of the body but not sin as
> well which is the death of the soul, anathema sit. (Let him be
> anathema.) For he contradicts the words of the apostle: "Sin
> came into the world through one man, and death through sin,
> and so death spread to all men as all sinned in him."[15]

Rahner agrees that death is something which ought not to
be. It is the essence of human nature to reach out to eternal

life. Since death is the extinction of life, it is the arch-contradiction of all that human beings are meant to be.

Rahner understands that because of sin human beings exist in a state of disorder. The integration and basic unity which human beings were meant to experience has been shattered and disrupted by sin. Because of sin, human beings experience disorder and antagonism against themselves, others, the world and God.

The distintegration we experience in our hearts, our lives, and in our relationships with God and others is the result of sin. Rahner calls this disintegration "concupiscence" and says:

> Death is the culmination of concupiscence; concupiscence is the appearance of the continuous presence of death in the reality of human life which spreads its veil of darkness over the whole of life.[16]

Death is the experience of our own disorder and limitations. Death is the supreme disintegration. Death is darkness.

In this regard, it is important to emphasize that Rahner understands death as an experience that is present throughout our lives and not just something we encounter at life's end. Rahner says that whenever human beings act freely against the essence of what it means to be human, we experience the darkness which we experience fully in death.

Like death, there is much in life that ought not to be. Rahner's understanding of death as an ever present experience of darkness helps us to understand the disorder we experience in our present life. The presence of darkness and disorder permeates the totality of human existence.

In the Second Vatican Council, the church teaches:

> It is in the face of death that the riddle of human existence becomes most acute; not only is man tormented by pain and by the advancing deterioration of his body, but even more so by a dread of perpetual extinction.[17]

But there is another aspect of death, Rahner says, that gives human beings hope. Rahner says that death can only be understood in the light of Christ's' death. By his death and resurrection, Jesus Christ assumed the totality of human experience. The word of God, united to Jesus Christ, became part of the world and the whole material order, thus transforming creation and transforming human death.

Rahner holds that in Christ, death was transformed from a manifestation of sin into a revelation of grace:

> The real miracle of Christ's death resides precisely in this: death, which can be experienced only as the advent of emptiness as the dead-end of sin, as the darkness of eternal night (especially since the supernatural order is the real order in which there should be no death), and which could be suffered, even by Christ himself, only as a state of being abandoned by God, now, through being embraced by the obedient "yes" of the Son, while losing nothing of the horror of divine abandonment native to death, is transformed into something completely different: into the advent of God in the midst of that empty loneliness into the manifestation of a complete, obedient surrender of the whole man to the Holy God at the very moment when man seems lost and far removed from him.[18]

Rahner says that it is the task of those today who seek to understand the meaning of death to proclaim the presence of hope in our lives because of the transformation of death by Christ.

Human beings experience death not just passively as an event coming from outside ourselves over which we have no control. Death is also experienced actively. Human beings experience death as the active self-surrender of self. Rahner says that although it is of the essence of human beings to surrender to incomprehensible mystery, it is only through hope that we can tear ourselves away from the feeling of abandonment.[19]

It is through Christ's death that we are able to surrender ourselves to the darkness of death in the hope that there is someone to whom we are surrendering ourselves. It is Christ who gives us hope.

The church teaches today that

> ... by his incarnation, the Son of God has united himself in some fashion with every man. He worked with human hands, thought with a human mind, acted by human choice, and loved with a human heart. Born of the Virgin Mary, he has truly been made one of us, like us in all things except sin.
>
> As an innocent lamb he merited life for us by the free shedding of his own blood. In him God reconciled us to himself and among ourselves. From bondage to the devil and sin, he delivered us, so that each one of us can say with the Apostle: the Son of God "loved me and gave himself up for me" (Gal 2:20). By suffering for us he not only provided us with an example for our imitation. He blazed a trail, and if we follow it, life and death are made holy and take on a new meaning.[20]

In our world today which so often teaches the lessons of self-centeredness as the key to fullness of life, we must dare to say that the secret of life—and death—is giving oneself away. We were meant to be gifts. Our God has gifted us with himself, and if we wish to achieve fulfillment we, too, must give ourselves away.

The council fathers note that man is the only creature on earth who "cannot fully find himself except through a sincere gift of himself."[21]

Christ has already "blazed the trail for us." Christ has already experienced the darkness of human death. He has cried out, "My God, my God, why have you abandoned me?" But he has also surrendered himself, united to all of human reality, to a loving Father to whom he dared to say, "Father, into your hands I commend my spirit."

If we understand death as a reality that is present throughout our lives, we will see that we are called to live lives of self-surrender, trusting that there is someone hidden in the darkness who makes sense out of all reality—and that that someone calls us by name.

Rahner is in agreement with the teachings of the church that death is a punishment for sin. The punishment is human disorder and disintegration which culminates in the total disintegration of death. Rahner's theology of death is in accord with the teaching of the church that Christ has transformed death and gives it new meaning. Rahner says that through Christ we discover in our present life that death has been changed into life, and that our condemnation has been changed into the visible advent of the kingdom of God.[22]

The church teaches:

> Through Christ and in Christ, the riddles of sorrow and death grow meaningful. Apart from his gospel, they overwhelm us. Christ has risen, destroying death by his death. He has lavished life upon us so that as sons in the Son, we can cry out in the Spirit: Abba, Father![23]

Purgatory

We have seen that the doctrine of purgatory has had a place in the thinking of the Christian community since very early in the history of the church. The practice of praying for the dead appears to have developed early in Christian practice. The doctrine of purgatory was first defined at the Councils of Lyons (1241) and Florence (1439).

In the Council of Trent, in the year 1563, the church defined the doctrine of purgatory in relation to the Protestant Reformers' rejection of the idea of an intermediate state between death and final perfection. The council fathers said:

> The Catholic Church, by the teaching of the Holy Spirit, in accordance with Sacred Scripture and the ancient tradition of the Fathers, has taught in the holy councils, and most recently in this ecumenical council, that there is a purgatory and that the souls detained there are helped by the prayers of the faithful and especially by the acceptable sacrifice of the altar.[24]

We have previously noted that Karl Rahner states his difficulty with the idea of purgatory as an intermediate period between the death of an individual and his final perfection. For Rahner, death is that final act in which a person decides for or against God forever. Rahner holds that the single and total perfecting of the human being in body and soul takes place immediately at death. Therefore, Rahner says that it is not possible to think of purgatory as an intermediate state where human beings are capable of changing the decision made for or against God in death.[25]

The image of purgatory as a "little hell" in which we painfully atone for our sins is also rejected by Rahner. Rahner notes that statements like these are statements which modern man feels are just forms of mythology and that he is no longer able to believe them in all seriousness.[26]

Rahner, however, does not reject the doctrine of purgatory. The idea of an interval, whether conceived of as purgatory or envisioned as a series of reincarnations as held in many other religious systems, reveals, says Rahner, the human desire for continuous integration and maturation.[27]

Rahner understands purgatory as a process of integration of the many dimensions of the total human being into the final decision made in death. In this integration, not only does the final decision permeate the many levels of the human being, but Rahner understands purgatory as the integration of the person into the whole of the material order. Rahner understands purgatory as the integration of the person, "as a constant and determining factor, into the world as a whole. . . . "[28]

Purgatory can best be understood in the light of Rahner's understanding of the all-cosmic relationship with the world into which human beings enter in death. In death human beings break out of the space-time limitations of the physical body. But because human beings are made up of spirit and matter, the person enters into a relationship with the material order in which finite spirit expresses itself. In the all-cosmic dimension the person has the "power or capacity of free and unhampered relations toward everything."[29]

Death marks the end of a specific stage in the development of human beings—the dimension of time and space. But death is not the final stage. In death, human beings enter into a more open relationship to the totality of the material order. In this stage, the human being

> ... experiences the contradiction between the divinely or-dained nature of his own being or that of the world on the one hand and that which still is through the still surviving effects of his own acts, in which his guilt has been objectified. He experiences these as the painful and punitive consequences of sin. Now the painful process by which this contradiction is overcome is his purgatory.[30]

Rahner, then, understands purgatory as a stage in the on-going development of finite spirit. Rahner notes that this un-derstanding of purgatory "excludes neither man's further de-velopment after death, nor suggests a lifeless concept of the future life with God."[31]

But how does the teaching of the church today on purga-tory compare with Rahner's understanding? And does the idea of purgatory have any meaning for us today?

It is important to note that in the teaching of the church, purgatory has never been defined as a place, nor as the image of a purging by fire ever been upheld by the church. The church has taught that there is a purging which takes place after death and that the prayers of those still alive help those who have died.

The image of purgatory as a place where disembodied souls suffer torments is drawn from a world-view which under-stood reality as a three-layer universe. In biblical and medi-eval times, reality was thought of as consisting of heaven, the world, and the underworld. If one were not in heaven, or the world, the only place to be was the underworld.

Today the church teaches that our understanding of reality and man's place in that reality has radically changed. In the Second Vatican Council, the council fathers point out:

Today's spiritual agitation and the changing conditions of life are part of a broader and deeper revolution. . . . History itself speeds along on so rapid a course that an individual person can scarcely keep abreast of it. The destiny of the human community has become all of a piece where once the various groups of men had a kind of private history of their own. Thus, the human race has passed from a rather static concept of reality to a more dynamic evolutionary one.[32]

Not only are human beings becoming increasingly aware of our ties with all of humankind, but our whole idea of reality is radically changing.

In the first quarter of this century two momentous theories were proposed: the theory of relativity and the quantum theory. From them sprang most of twentieth century physics. But the new physics revealed more than simply a better model of the physical world. Physicists began to realize that their discoveries demanded a radical reformulation of the most fundamental aspects of reality.

Many ordinary people, too, searching for a deeper meaning behind their lives, find their beliefs about the world very much in tune with the new physics. The physicists' outlook is even finding sympathy with psychologists and sociologists, especially those who advocate a holistic approach to their subjects.[33]

The quantum theory and the theory of relativity contain significant insight into the nature of the material order. These theories describe reality in such a way that emphasis is put on the individual wholeness of the material order. Reality is not a collection of separate things but a network of relations which is involved in dynamic movement and development. These theories must be taken into account in our contemporary understanding of who human beings are. We are part, say the scientists, of a material order which is a network of relations involved in dynamic movement and development.

In the face of this changing understanding of who human beings are and what the world is, the church teaches:

> The people of God believes that it is led by the Spirit of the Lord, who fills the earth. Motivated by this faith, it labors to decipher authentic signs of God's presence and purpose in the happenings, needs, and aspirations in which this people has a part along with other men of our age. For faith throws a new light on everything, manifests God's design for man's total vocation, and thus directs the mind to solutions which are fully human

When we examine the signs of the times, we find in today's world the presence of disorder and the longing for integration. The church teaches:

> The truth is that the imbalances under which the modern world labors are limited with that more basic imbalance rooted in the heart of man. For in man himself many elements wrestle with one another. Thus, on the one hand, as a creature he experiences his limitations in a multitude of ways. On the other, he feels himself to be boundless in his desires and summoned to a higher life.[35]

Perhaps the reason that the past image of purgatory so emphasized the plight of the individual soul was the emergence of individualism and the stress on the role and identity of the individual in western society. In contemporary society a new awareness of the person's solidarity with the world and the interrelatedness of all creation have emerged. These insights are reflected in Rahner's understanding of purgatory and the church's teaching on the contemporary signs of the times.

Today the modern person understands that he/she is multidimensional. Furthermore, contemporary pyschological insights have revealed that the integration and harmonization of the many levels of the person is not an easy task.

Since Rahner understands our images of what happened after death as images which reveal the "inner moment of man and of his actual being as it is present to him now,"[36] we may say that Rahner's understanding of purgatory as a process of integration is in tune with the contemporary person's experience of life.

It may also be said that Rahner's understanding of purgatory is compatible with the church's teaching on purgatory as a purifying process and the church's teaching on our changing understanding of reality and humankind's place in the world.

Rahner's understanding of purgatory is also compatible with the church's teaching on the benefits of the prayers of the faithful for those who have died. In Rahner's understanding of the all-cosmic dimension which we enter into on death, those still alive and those who have died continue to be in relationship through their relationship with the material order.

Purgatory is not a far-off place where we go after death to pay off our spiritual debts. Purgatory is the painful process of the integration and harmonization of creation which, once disrupted by sin, now has been assumed by Christ. We, united in Christ, are part of this cosmic process. It is a present reality which we now experience painfully as a human community, but it is a reality which has already been achieved for us by Christ.

The church teaches:

> Indeed, the Lord Jesus, when he prayed to the Father "that they all may be one . . . as we are one" (Jn 17:21–22), opened up vistas closed to human reason.[37]

The process may be painful, but the unity to which we are called will lead us to vistas closed to human reason.

Hell

There may be some who think that according to the teachings of the church, "You're dammed if you do and dammed if you don't."

The church teaches that hell does indeed exist. It also teaches that entry into hell takes place immediately at death.

The doctrine of hell was taught by the church in the Synod of Constantinople (543), the Fourth Lateran Council (1215) and the Council of Florence (1442).

In 1336, Benedict XII in the constitution *Benedictus Deus* said:

> We define that according to the general disposition of God the souls of those who die in actual mortal sin go down immediately after death into hell and are tormented by the pains of hell.[38]

In our world today, hell is not a popular topic of discussion and many of us are indeed grateful for a church that no longer puts the "fear of hell" into us. Hans Küng in *Eternal Life?* notes that in a survey taken in Germany in 1967, seventy-eight percent of Protestants and forty-seven percent of Catholics said they did not believe in the existence of hell. By 1980, eighty-three percent of Protestants and fifty-nine percent of Catholics said they no longer believed in hell.[39] Is there a hell and does it have any significance for us today?

Hell is spoken of in the New Testament. In the gospel of Matthew, Jesus tells the parable of the weeds among the wheat. In the parable, the weeds are the followers of the evil one, the devil. The harvest is the end of the world. Jesus tells his disciples that just as weeds are collected and burned, so too the Son of Man shall send his angels to collect the evildoers, and "they will throw them into the fiery furnace, where there will be wailing and grinding of teeth" (Mt 13:42).

In the story of the last judgment, Jesus says that the Son of Man will tell those who have not served him, "Depart from me, you accursed, into the eternal fire prepared for the devil and his angels" (Mt 25:41).

And in teaching his disciples on what lengths they should go to, to avoid hell, the gospel of Matthew has Jesus say:

If your right eye causes you to sin, tear it out and throw it away. It is better for you to lose one of your members than to have your whole body thrown into Gehenna. And if your right hand causes you to sin, cut it off and throw it away. It is better for to lose one of your members than to have your whole body go into Gehenna (Mt 5:29–30).

Rahner notes the times in the New Testament that Jesus refers to hell as a place of punishment. He points out, first, that these passages must be understood in the light of their literary character as "threat discourses." Various literary forms were used by the authors of the Old and New Testament in order to get across a certain message to their audience. The authors used poetry, drama, and sometimes speeches filled with invective. This does not mean, Rahner reminds us, that Jesus was speaking of a literal place or recommending actual physical mutilation.

Secondly, Rahner points out that these scriptural references to hell and Christ's teaching on hell must be interpreted as indicating only the "possibility" of eternal damnation. While our salvation in Jesus Christ has already been accomplished, whether or not many persons or even one person will actually be condemned to hell must be thought of as a possibility, not as a certainty.

The real significance of the doctrine of hell, Rahner maintains, is not the image it provides of torments in another world. Our understanding of hell "must apply itself above all to bringing out the real relevance of the affirmation of hell to human existence."[40]

In Rahner's understanding, hell must be understood as the drive toward self-autonomy. Human beings are endowed with freedom. Rahner defines human freedom as the power to decide that which is to be final and definitive in one's life. It is through our freedom that we either accept or rebel against that which is of the essence of our creaturehood, that is, self-surrender to the incomprehensible mystery which is God. Every moment of our life is a stage on the way to this final

goal of total self-surrender. Life can be an act of faith in which
we free ourselves into the hands of God or, says Rahner, life
can be an "act of desperately clinging, of protest, of despair, of
force expressed in the pride of seeking one's own absolute
autonomy."[41]

Hell must not be thought of as a place of punishment which
awaits human beings in the future. In Rahner's thought hell
exists on a cosmic scale even now. The drive toward self-
autonomy is a contradiction of the essence of what it means to
be human; it is also a contradiction of all that creation is
meant to be, since, as Rahner notes, Christ's death and resurrection had established an order of salvation for all creation.[42]

Hell is the antithesis of everything that God's creation is
meant to be. In our time, the church, too, has shifted its emphasis on hell as a place of punishment which awaits us after
death, to an emphasis on the effects of hell which can be felt in
our lives now. The doctrine of hell was certainly not a central
theme of the Second Vatican Council. But the council fathers
did speak of the "monumental struggle against the powers of
darkness (which) pervades the whole history of man. The bat-
tle was joined from the very origins of the world and will
continue until the last day as the Lord has attested. Caught in
this conflict man is obliged to wrestle constantly if he is to
cling to what is good. Nor can he achieve his own integrity
without valiant efforts and the help of God's grace."[43]

The council fathers note that today that the desire for human independence is such that many find difficulty with any
kind of dependence on God.[44]

Whenever human beings deny their dependence on God,
the council fathers say, "At the same time, man becomes out
of harmony with himself, with others and with all created
things. Therefore, man is split within himself."[45]

Both Rahner and the contemporary teaching of the church
choose not to speak of hell in traditional images of fire, de-
mons, and howls of pain. It may be said that Rahner is in
agreement with the teaching of the church that hell is the
drive toward self-autonomy or independence from God. The

results of this drive toward darkness are already evident in our human experience. The council fathers point out:

> . . . whatever is opposed to life itself, such as any type of murder, genocide, abortion, euthanasia, or willful self-destruction, whatever violates the integrity of the human person, such as mutilation, torments inflicted on the body or mind, attempts to coerce the will itself, whatever insults human dignity, such as subhuman living conditions, arbitrary imprisonment, deportation, slavery, prostitution, the selling of women and children, as well as disgraceful working conditions, where men are treated as mere tools for profit, rather than as free and responsible persons—such things and others of their ilk are infamous indeed. They poison human society.[46]

It is perhaps much easier to imagine hell as a far-away place, but the church reminds us that the effects of self-centeredness which exist on an individual and global scale are indeed very real, and the effects of this drive poison human society.

This understanding of hell is much more menacing. Hell is now and hell can be forever. We have the power to set ourselves in contradiction, in all the dimensions of our being, to be finally lost and estranged from ourselves, from the community of humankind, from the cosmos, and from God. We may choose to live the alienation and antagonism which is hell right now.

Judgment

The church teaches that there are two types of judgment, the particular judgment and the general judgment. The doctrine of the particular judgment is implied although not stated explicitly in the Second General Council of Lyons (1274). The council states that those who die go immediately to heaven, hell, or purgatory, thus implying that some kind of individual or particular judgment has taken place. Pope Benedict XII, in the constitution "Benedictus Deus" (1336), also teaches that at death all who have departed this world are assigned to heaven, hell or purgatory.

Concerning the teaching of the church on the general judgment, the Fourth Lateran Council stated that when Christ

> . . . will come at the end of the world, he will judge the living and the dead, and he will reward all, both the lost and the elect, according to their works.[47]

Karl Rahner agrees with the teaching of the church that there is a particular and general judgment. But the real importance of its teaching, says Rahner, is to show the relationships between the individual and all of humankind. The church teaches that there is an individual judgment to emphasize the importance of each person's responsibility for his/her own actions. The general judgment, says Rahner, "speaks of the fact that mankind and its history, as a collective unity, comes under God's judgment."[48]

But, says Rahner, we need to emphasize more in our understanding of the particular and general judgment that the fate of the individual and the collective destiny of the world are irrevocably interrelated.

When we study eschatology (or the last things—death, heaven, hell, purgatory, and judgment), Rahner says, we can really only understand eschatology as an individual person from the perspective of the final destiny of the world. The fate of the individual depends on the outcome of the whole of the world, and, vice versa, the outcome of the whole of the world depends on the destiny of the individuals who are part of it.

We understand our judgment, then, from the perspective not only of our own personal history but from the perspective of our relationship to the collective sphere of being to which we belong. We are part of human history.

Rahner also understands judgment as something which we experience now and not just at the end of our lives or at the end of the world. Rahner says that all humankind constantly judges itself in the light of God's presence among us. Rahner understands judgment in the sense we read of it in John's gospel.

> For God did not send his Son into the world to condemn the world, but that the world might be saved through him. Whoever believes in him will not be condemned, but whoever does not believe has already been condemned, because he has not believed in the name of the only Son of God. And this is the verdict, that the light came into the world, but people preferred the darkness to light, because their works were evil (Jn 3:17–19).

It is the light of God's presence which serves as the standard by which we, as individuals and as all humankind, are judged.

In the Constitution on the Church in the Modern World, the church teaches:

> The truth is that only in the mystery of the Incarnate Word does the mystery of man take on light. For Adam, the first man, was a figure of him who was to come, namely, Christ the Lord. Christ the final Adam, by the revelation of the mystery of the Father and of his love, fully reveals man to man himself and makes his supreme calling clear.[49]

The traditional eschatology of the church has been a futuristic theology. The church taught about the last things as events which would occur in the future. We see in the teaching of the church in the Second Vatican Council a shift in perspective toward a *realized* eschatology. Karl Rahner's eschatology may also be understood as a realized eschatology. We say that Rahner's eschatology is a *realized* eschatology because in Rahner's understanding the final transformation of creation has already taken place or been realized. The word has become flesh and has already become the innermost life not only of human beings but of all creation. The word of God has become part of human history. While we human beings are free and responsible for the working out of our history, our final destiny has been assured. Christ is the salvation of creation. Our final destiny is Christ.

Rahner holds that the more we understand our final destiny, the more we understand ourselves and our present reality. Our understanding of who human beings are must *begin* from the perspective that humankind is already united with the incarnate word. It is in the light of this union that we are judged.

In the Second Vatican Council the church teaches very practical ways on how we will be judged. The council fathers note that we are living in an era of profound and rapid changes in the social, pyschological, and moral order. In such a world, the church teaches:

> The joys and the hopes, the griefs and the anxieties of the men of this age, especially those who are poor or in any way afflicted, these too are the joys and hopes, the griefs and anxieties of the followers of Christ. Indeed, nothing genuinely human fails to raise an echo in their hearts.[50]

Rahner's understanding of judgment is in accord with the teaching of the church. Judgment is a reality that is present now in our lives.

> Now is the time of judgment on this the world; now the ruler of this world will be driven out. And when I am lifted up from the earth I will draw everyone to myself. . . . Walk while you have the light, so that darkness may not overcome you. Whoever walks in the dark does not know where he is going. While you have the light believe in the light, so that you may become children of the light (Jn 12:31–36).

The Second Coming of Christ

The church teaches that at the end of time Christ will come again in glory.[51]

In the gospels, the second coming of Christ is described as the coming of the Son of Man in glory, with angels and power. The second coming is preceded by signs in the heavens. The second coming will be like a flash of lightning. At this time, Christ will be enthroned and rule at the right hand of God. The second coming of Christ will establish the reign of Christ for a thousand years.

The question concerning the time and the date of the return of Jesus Christ in the second coming has been a topic of debate since the beginning of the church. When it became clear to the early Christian community that the second coming of Christ was not as imminent as they had first supposed, different interpretations concerning the return of Christ developed in the church.

Some held that the passage in the book of Revelation which states that Christ will reign for a thousand years meant that the church would reign on earth for a thousand years after he had returned. This view is called the pre-millennialist view.

Others held that the thousand year reign of Christ was already in progress and that Christ would return at its end. This view is called the post-millennialist view.

Rahner holds that to speculate about the time and the date of the second coming is to miss the meaning of this image. Rahner says that what the image of the second coming of Christ reveals is the permanent blessed presence of Christ in human history.[52]

We have seen that Rahner emphasizes the hope that the image of the second coming of Christ gives. This image, says Rahner, gives meaning to our existence now. For by it we understand "the unfathomable depth and richness of our existence."[53]

This proclamation that God is with us in Christ is what ultimately makes life meaningful. It is this hope that life is meaningful which, Rahner says, "must be impressed on secular life."[54]

The church, too, teaches that our expectation of the second

coming of Christ in glory cannot diminish our responsibility
for the present.

> . . . man is called as a son to commune with God and to share
> in his happiness. She (the Church) further teaches that a hope
> related to the end of time does not diminish the importance of
> intervening duties, but rather underguides the acquittal of
> them with fresh incentive. By contrast, when a divine substruc-
> ture and the hope of life eternal are wanting, man's dignity is
> most grievously lacerated, as current events often attest. The
> riddles of life and death, of guilt and grief go unsolved, with the
> frequent result that men succumb to despair.[55]

The "divine substructure" to which the council fathers refer
would be explained by Rahner as the "very essential and real
presence of Christ" in human history and the world.[56]
    While Rahner understands the second coming of Christ as a
present awareness of the transformation of humankind and
creation, he also says:

> The meaning and significance of the present is based on the
> hopeful openness to the approach to the absolute future. (Chris-
> tianity) . . . is the proclamation of an absolute becoming which
> does not continue into emptiness but really attains the abso-
> lute future, which is indeed already moving within it . . . the
> real nature of man can therefore be defined as precisely the
> possibility of attaining the absolute future.[57]

The real meaning of what it means to be human is unending becoming. Humankind and creation are united with the
incarnate word in the unending quest toward that infinite
horizon which is absolute future.
    Rahner's interpretation of the second coming of Christ
maintains a balance in the understanding of the eminence
and transcendence of God. By the second coming of Christ we
may correctly understand that through Christ God has become immanent or part of our human history and yet at the
same time we are now part of a destiny which absolutely

transcends our human history. Rahner's understanding also stresses the intrinsic value of the material order and man's responsibility for it. Christ has come to take on human history, but man as free subject is still responsible for his history. In the past, the church has had little to say about what actually would happen at the end of the world. However in the documents of the Second Vatican Council, the church teaches that in the glory of heaven all things will be transformed.

> Then the human race as well as the entire world, which is intimately related to man and achieves its purpose through him, will be perfectly reestablished in Christ.[58]

Rahner holds that the transformed earth and heaven which is the destiny of humankind is the culmination of a process in which spirit and matter have been united since the beginning of time. While this final transformation, according to Rahner, has already been achieved in the risen Jesus Christ, it is hidden from us now.[59] There will be a final transformation, says Rahner, when the hidden glory of the risen Christ breaks through and manifests itself in the material order. Then, all of creation will achieve its final destiny. The material order will achieve the destiny begun for it by the eternal word of God who wedded heaven to earth. Then the earth, the sun, the stars, and all humankind will be "risen as he said."

Rahner says that resurrection is our ultimate form, the form for which we were created,

> . . . the transfiguration of the end. Time, therefore, means the resurrection of the individual, and a new earth, and a new heaven.[60]

The church teaches in the words of the Second Vatican Council:

> We know neither the moment of the consummation of the earth and of man nor the way the universe will be transformed.

The form of this world, distorted by sin, is a new dwelling and a new earth in which righteousness dwells, whose happiness will fill and surpass all the desires of peace arising in the hearts of men. Then with death conquered the sons of God will be raised in Christ, and what was sown in weakness and dishonor will put on the imperishable: charity and its works will remain and all of creation, which God made for man, will be set free from its bondage to decay.

We have been warned, of course, that it profits man nothing if he gains the whole world and loses or forfeits himself. Far from diminishing our concern to develop this earth, the expectancy of a new earth should spur us on, for it is here that the body of a new human family grows, foreshadowing in some way the age which is to come. That is why, although we must be careful to distinguish earthly progress clearly from the increase of the kingdom of Christ, such progress is of vital concern to the kingdom of God, insofar as it can contribute to the better ordering of human society.

When we have spread on earth the fruits of our nature and our enterprise—human dignity, brotherly communion, and freedom—according to the command of the Lord and his Spirit, we will find them once again, cleansed this time from the stain of sin, illuminated and transfigured, when Christ presents to his Father an eternal and universal kingdom "of truth and life, a kingdom of holiness and grace, a kingdom of justice, love and peace." Here on earth the kingdom is mysteriously present; when the Lord came it will enter into its perfection.[61]

Then all creation will sing,

Rejoice, heavenly powers! Sing, choirs of angels!
    Exult, all creation around God's throne!
    Jesus Christ, our King, is risen!
    Sound the trumpet of salvation!

Rejoice, O earth, in shining splendor,
    radiant in the brightness of your King!
    Christ has conquered! Glory fills you!
    Darkness vanishes for ever![62]

NOTES

1. J. Neuner and J. Depuis, ed., *The Christian Faith in the Doctrinal Documents of the Catholic Church* (New York: Alba House, 1982), pp. 13, 118, 120, 124, 126.

2. Karl Rahner, "The Body in the Order of Salvation," *Theological Investigations*, Vol. 17, translated by Margaret Kohl (London: Darton, Longman, and Todd, 1981), pp. 83–84.

3. Leo J. O'Donovan, ed., "Hope for Humanity: Rahner's Eschatology," by William Thompson, *A World of Grace* (New York: The Seabury Press, 1980).

4. Walter M. Abbott, S.J. (ed.), "The Pastoral Constitution on the Church in the Modern World," #18, *The Documents of Vatican II* (New Jersey: New Centry Publishers, 1966), p. 215.

5. Ibid., #5, pp. 203–204.

6. Ibid., #3, p. 200.

7. Ibid., #19, p. 213.

8. Karl Rahner, "The Theological Problems Entailed in the Idea of the New Earth," *Theological Investigations*, Vol. 10, translated by David Bourke (London: Darton, Longman, and Todd, 1973), p. 266.

9. Walter Abbott, S.J., op. cit., #4, p. 203.

10. Ibid.

11. National Conference of Catholic Bishops, *The Challenge of Peace: God's Promise and Our Response* (United States Catholic Conference, 1983), p. 40.

12. Karl Rahner, "The Theological Problems Entailed in the Idea of the New Earth," *Theological Investigations*, Vol. 10, op. cit., p. 261.

13. Karl Rahner, "A Fragmentary Evaluation of the Concept of the Future," *Theological Investigations*, Vol. 10, op. cit., p. 261.

14. Karl Rahner, *The Foundations of the Christian Faith*, translated by William V. Dych (New York: Seabury Press, 1978), p. 433.

15. J. Neuner, S.J., and J. Dupuis, S.J., *The Christian Faith*, op. cit., p. 138.

16. Karl Rahner, *On the Theology of Death*, translated by Charles H. Henkey (New York: Herder and Herder, 1965), p. 57.

17. Walter M. Abbott, S.J., op. cit., #18, p. 215.

18. Karl Rahner, *On the Theology of Death*, op. cit., p. 78.

19. Karl Rahner, "On the Theology of Death," *Theological Investigations*, Vol. 13, translated by David Bourke (London: Darton, Longman, and Todd, 1975), p. 182.

20. Walter M. Abbott, S.J., op. cit., #22, pp. 220–221.
21. Ibid., #24, p. 223.
22. Karl Rahner, *On the Theology of Death*, op. cit., p. 80.
23. Walter M. Abbott, S.J., op. cit., #22, p. 222.
24. E.J. Fortman, S.J., *Everlasting Life After Death* (New York: Alba House, 1976), p. 133.
25. Karl Rahner, *On the Theology of Death*, op. cit., p. 35.
26. Gerald A. McCool (ed.), *A Rahner Reader* (New York: The Seabury Press, 1975), p. 173.
27. Karl Rahner, *The Foundations of the Christian Faith*, op. cit., p. 442.
28. Karl Rahner, *On the Theology of Death*, op. cit., p. 71.
29. Ibid., p. 34.
30. Karl Rahner, "A Brief Study on Indulgences," *Theological Investigations*, Vol. 10, op. cit., p. 65.
31. Karl Rahner, *On the Theology of Death*, op. cit., pp. 35–36.
32. Walter M. Abbott, S.J., op. cit., #5, p. 204.
33. Paul Davies, *God and the New Physics* (New York: Simon and Schuster, 1983), p. 3.
34. Walter M. Abbott, S.J., op. cit., #5, p. 204.
35. Ibid., #10, p. 207.
36. Karl Rahner, "The Hermeneutics of Eschatological Assertions," *Theological Investigations*, Vol. 4, p. 331.
37. Walter J. Abbott, S.J., op. cit., #24, p. 223.
38. Denzinger and Schöenmetzer, cited in Hans Küng's *Eternal Life?* (New York: Doubleday and Company, Inc., 1982), p. 131.
39. Ibid., p. 137.
40. Karl Rahner (ed.), "Hell," *Sacramentum Mundi: An Encyclopedia of Theology*, 6 volumes (New York: Seabury Press, 1968–1970), Vol. 3, p. 7.
41. Gerald A. McCool (ed.), "On Christian Dying," *A Rahner Reader*, op. cit., pp. 355–356.
42. Karl Rahner, *On the Theology of Death*, op. cit., p. 74.
43. Walter M. Abbott, S.J., op. cit., p. 235.
44. Ibid., #19, p. 216.
45. Ibid., #13, p. 211.
46. Ibid., #27, p. 226.
47. E.J. Fortman, *Everlasting Life After Death*, op. cit., p. 253.
48. Karl Rahner, "Particular Judgment," *Sacramentum Mundi*, Vol. 3, op. cit., p. 275.

49. Walter M. Abbott, S.J., op. cit., #22, p. 220.

50. Ibid., #1, p. 199.

51. See Mt 16:27/ Mk 18:38/ Lk. 9:29; Mt 24:30/ Mk 13:26/ Lk 21:27; Mt 24:29/ Mk 13:24/ Lk 21:25–27; Mt 13:41/ Mk 14:62/ Lk 22:69; Rev 20:1–6.

52. Karl Rahner, "Parousia," *Theological Investigations*, Vol. 4, translated by Kevin Smyth (Baltimore: Helicon Press, 1966), p. 345.

53. Karl Rahner, "Eternity from Time," *Practice of Faith, A Handbook of Contemporary Spirituality* (New York: Crossroad, 1983), p. 311.

54. Karl Rahner, "Theological Problems Entailed in the Idea of a New Earth," *Theological Investigations*, Vol. 10, op. cit., p. 260.

55. Walter M. Abbott, S.J., op. cit., #21, p. 218.

56. Karl Rahner, "Hidden Victory," *Theological Investigations*, Vol. 7, translated by David Burke (New York: Herder and Herder, 1971), p. 157.

57. Karl Rahner, "Marxist Utopia and the Christian Future of Man," *Theological Investigations*, Vol. 6 (New York: Seabury Press, 1974), p. 60.

58. Walter M. Abbott, S.J., op. cit., #48, pp. 78–79.

59. Karl Rahner, "Jesus' Resurrection," *Theological Investigations*, Vol. 17, translated by Margaret Kohl (London: Darton, Longman and Todd, 1981), p. 19.

60. Karl Rahner, "Some Implications of the Scholastic Concept of Uncreated Grace." *Theological Investigations*, Vol. 1, translated by Cornelius Ernst, O.P. (Baltimore: Helicon Press, 1963), p. 319.

61. Walter M. Abbott, S.J., op. cit., #39, p. 237.

62. Catholic Biblical Association, "Short Form of the Easter Proclamation," *Lectionary for Mass* (New York: Catholic Book Publishing Co., 1970, p. 185.

6

Toward an American Theology of Death

It is never easy to die. In some sense it is particularly difficult for Americans to totally surrender themselves to incomprehensible mystery. The typical American folk-hero is the rugged individual, the person who depends on no one and who makes it on his own.

The roots of our particular American brand of individualism may be traced back to the foundations of our country. America was founded to be a "city set on a hill," a beacon light for all the world to see. The founders of our nation were a group of church reformers who had despaired of purifying the Church of England. These Puritans, as they were called, established Massachusetts Bay colony in 1630. The colony was characterized by strong clerical leadership and a religiously regulated society. Although the Puritans had come to the new world to enjoy religious freedom, they rejected those who did not embrace their religion and even limited political rights to only those who belonged to their church.

By 1645 the Puritans had established a theocracy. A theocracy is a state which is governed by individuals who are believed to be directly guided by God. Many scholars attribute the development of democracy in America to the way of life established by the Puritans. The Puritans were absolutely convinced that they had been called by God as a people to establish a new Jerusalem on the face of the earth. However, David E. Stannard notes that while "the Puritans' sense of *national* mission was infused with an overwhelming and single-minded confidence, their sense of *individual* salvation was beset with agonizing insecurity."[1]

Puritans believed that because of Adam's sin all humankind had become totally depraved and absolutely alienated from God. It is difficult for us today to conceive of the Puritan understanding of total personal decadence. While the Puritans believed that all persons were called to serve God in the world in the best way they knew how, they also believed that only a few persons had been predestined for salvation. These few elect would enjoy the pleasures of heaven, while all the rest would be condemned to the tortures of hell for all eternity. Salvation or damnation was not the result of a good life or good works, but depended entirely on the arbitrary whim of a distant God. One famous Puritan theologian, Jonathan Edwards (1703–1758), said in a Sunday sermon that God held the eternal souls of the Puritans over the fires of hell as a spider held its prey by a string over its web.

The only indication one had of whether or not he/she was destined for eternal salvation was the experience of signs of grace. Therefore, the Puritans constantly examined their minds and hearts in an effort to detect signs of God's presence. This preoccupation with determining if one had received the Spirit led to a terrible introspection and a concentration on one's individual outcome. It also created an overwhelming fear of dying. Writing in 1723, Cotton Mather, a Puritan leader, described death as the "King of Terrors."[2]

The Puritans understood that at death the destiny of the soul was eternally decided. Therefore, they had little concern for the corpse which remained. In the early days of the New England colonies, the 1630s–1640s, the bodies of the deceased were disposed of quickly. The corpses were buried simply. No scripture was read nor sermon given. No tombstones marked the graves.

By the mid-1600s, a change in attitudes toward the dead

began to emerge. The Puritans who considered themselves a pilgrim people on journey home to God began to realize that they were going to be in America for a while. As commerce developed and emotional ties with England were severed, the colonies prospered. Puritans believed that one of the signs of grace was a prosperous life. As the prosperity of the Puritans became greater, the use of material things affected their funeral rites and customs. Elaborate funeral services were developed. Lengthy sermons were preached and costly tombstones were erected. A variety of paraphernalia was developed such as funeral rings, gloves, and cards to be used during the funeral services. But the accumulation of material objects could not conceal the fact that the terror of death was still there. An absolutely transcendent and sovereign God had already arbitrarily determined one's destiny.

In the eighteenth century a wave of religious fervor swept America. Enthusiasm movements which became known as the Great Awakenings stirred great emotional reactions. Preachers brought thousands to conversion by telling of the fires of hell and the terrors of damnation and ironically led to a reversal of attitudes toward dying and death.

By the eighteenth century a romantic and sentimental attitude toward death replaced the Puritan terror of death in America. A nostalgic and melodramatic longing for the peace and joy of death pervaded American attitudes. David E. Stannard quotes from eighteenth century poets who waxed eloquently on the fortunate dead.

> Absent from Flesh! O blissful Thought!
> What unknown Joys this Moment brings!
> Free'd from the Mischief sin hath wrought,
> From Pains, and Tears and all their Springs.
>
> *Absent from Flesh!* Illustrious Day!
> Surprising Scene! Triumphant Stroke!
> That rends the Prison of my Clay,
> And I can feel my Fetters broke!
>   (Josiah Smith "Doctrine and Glory
>   of the Saints' Resurrection," 1742)

I long to be within the Veil,
  And leave this House of Clay;
Oh for some burning Seraphs Wing;
  No longer would I stay.

My willing Mind obeys the Call,
  And meets Thee with Desire;
I long, I faint, to be with Thee,
  How can I longer bear?

Thus she is gone; her Pulse doth cease;
  We have her last Farewell;
Her glass is run; her sun is set;
  In heav'n she's gone to dwell.

But shall we mourn? Our Loss is great,
  Yet greater is her Bliss.
She's gone to dwell with Jesus Christ,
  And see him Face to Face!
      (Mary Williams "Dying Mother's
        Advice and Farewell,"1749)[3]

Death was so romanticized that tombstones often depicted happy cherubs and representations of the blissful
faithful departed.

By the nineteenth century, the sentimental image of death
began to give way to a more pragmatic attitude. Embalming
of the dead became a standard practice. The development of
funeral parlors, where the deceased was waked or watched
over until burial, gradually led to the commercialization of
the funeral industry. By the twentieth century, Jessica Mitford could write of the commercial practices which had developed in regard to the disposal of the dead in *The American
Way of Death*.[4] Dying and death had become big business in
the United States.

As we near the end of the twentieth century the development of complex medical care has again caused a major shift
in American attitudes toward dying and death. Not only do
most Americans now die in hospitals rather than at home,
elaborate methods for preserving and prolonging life have

raised the question of when life ends and death begins. Then, too, Americans are confronted as no other generation has been with the possibility of mass death and global annihilation because of nuclear arms.

In the face of these enormous issues, we must ask ourselves if Karl Rahner's understanding of death and life after death is helpful to us as Americans.

In order to develop a theology of death Americans must first talk about death as it truly is. In contemporary American society a certain "conspiracy of silence" seems to surround dying and death. Americans tend to deny death by taking elaborate care to stave off or decorate the aging process. We also tend to deny death by preventing those who are dying from talking about their approaching death. When friends and family members die, our funeral customs continue the conspiracy which denies death. The bodies of those who have died are cosmetically treated to appear alive. How often one hears that the deceased appears to be sleeping. The pain and finality of death are not really accepted.

In *Encounters with Silence,* Rahner prays about those who have died.

> They have gone away; they are silent. Not a word comes through from them; not a single sign of their gentle love and kindness comes to warm my heart. How awfully still the dead are, how *dead!*[5]

When we speak of death as "eternal rest or sleep" we are denying the stark reality of death. Too often we deny death by speaking of "life after death" rather than death itself. Rahner points out that persons "quickly turn to the question of what comes after death as though the theology of death can only begin there."[6]

Each of us will die. Each of us must confront the fact that death is real. There are no answers as to what death is really like for the individual. Death is the unanswerable question. Rahner says that human beings are questions which only God can answer.[7] Death is the question we have been asking all our lives. It is the profound question that has given direction and meaning to our lives. It is the unanswered query for which we have searched all our lives. It is not possible to put into words what this question is for each individual. The question is as unique to each person as fingerprints and cell structures. Each person is a question which is asked most fully in death. Death is God's answer to the question which we are. Accepting death as the unanswerable question is difficult for pragmatic Americans. We seek sure and swift solutions. Death is a question for which we have no answer.

When we reflect on death, we are invariably drawn to the conclusion that death is something that should not be. Each one of us asks, "Why must I die? Why must my loved ones die?" Death, as we experience it, is indeed something which should not be. We were made for life and love. Jesus told us, "I have come in order that you might have life—life in all its fullness" (Jn 10:10).

It is because of sin that we experience the terror and pain of death as we do. Before the sin of "Adam," human beings would have experienced death as a bodily transformation which would have been the culmination of life in space and time. Rahner says,

> This does not of course mean that if there were no original or personal sin man would have continued in perpetuity his bio logical life in time, or that before "Adam" there was no death in the animal kingdom. Even without sin man would have ended his biological, historical life in space and time, and would have entered into his definitive condition before God by means of a free act engaging his whole life. Death as we know it now, or part of man's constitution subject to concupiscence, in darkness, weakness and obscurity regarding its actual nature, is a consequence of sin.[8]

It is all right then to be afraid of death. We rightly fear the termination of our existence. All of us long to survive forever as the person we now experience ourselves as. Philosophical arguments about the survival of consciousness or the immortality of the soul do not convince us. Each of us asks in the depths of his or her heart, "Will I survive?"

Rahner says that death "is a human event concerning man as a whole and as a spiritual person, an event which concerns his very essence: his definitive, free, personal self-realization."[9]

Americans fear death as the annihilation of themselves. We, who have placed such emphasis in our history on the development and the rights of individuals, fear the obliteration of ourselves as individuals. But death does not demolish us. In death we achieve a "personal self-realization" which is not possible in life. For Americans who are accustomed to "being all you can be," this seems like a paradox. How can we achieve in death a personal self-realization which we cannot achieve in life? What is this self-realization?

Rahner says that death "is an active consummation from within brought about by the person himself, a maturing self-realization which embodies the result of what a man has made of himself during life, the achievement of total personal self-possession, a real effectuation of self, the fullness of freely produced personal reality."[10]

What life is really all about is the construction of a personal reality which is open to the infinite whom we call God. All of our life is an attempt to fashion this person we are meant to be and whose fullness is most completely expressed in our death.

Americans are often accused of being materialistic and are criticized for our seemingly endless quest for the accumulation of things. Perhaps what this endless craving reveals most about us is our aching longing for the infinite. Even the universe is not enough for us. We long for a final consummation of ourselves. We long to possess ourselves totally and to be authentically effective. We want to enjoy, as Rahner says, "the fullness of freely produced personal reality."

This person is most fully expressed in death. For this reason we must mediate frequently on our own death. As we have noted, Americans do not like to dwell on the subject of death.

But Rahner reminds us, "Knowledge, even if mostly an implicit knowledge, of the inevitability of death, though not of its when and where, intrinsically determines the whole of life."[11]

If we do not allow ourselves to think of our death or if death has no meaning for us, then neither will life. When death assumes meaning for us, then so does life.

We can only understand the real meaning of death in light of the death of Christ. When we ponder the mystery of the death of Jesus Christ on his cross, we must remember that his cross is also his throne. Through his death, Jesus Christ transformed not only all human death but also the destiny of the cosmos. By his death Jesus Christ became the destiny of all creation.

> To the innermost reality of the world there belongs what we call Jesus Christ in his life and death, what was poured out over the cosmos at the moment when the vessel of his body was shattered in death, and Christ actually became, even in his humanity, what he had always been by his dignity, the heart of the universe, the innermost centre of all created reality.[12]

By his death and resurrection Jesus Christ assumed all of human reality. Because of his death and resurrection, that human reality has forever been transformed. Human reality has been transformed so that the more we become the person we are meant to be the more we become part of Christ. The more the cosmos achieves its final destiny, the more personal it will become. All of the cosmos is becoming united in Christ.

> In all wisdom and insight, he has made known to us the mystery of his will in accord with his favor that he set forth in him as a plan for the fullness of times, to sum up all things in Christ in heaven and on earth (Ep 1:8–10).

In Christ, we are united to all of human reality. In Christ we have become part of all creation which is being gathered up as a perfect gift to the Father through the power of the Holy Spirit.

The bishops of the United States remind us: "Death should be depicted for what it is, the final opportunity to assent to the divine will and give oneself freely to God. Several stages have been identified in the process by which an individual typically comes to terms with the fact that he or she will die: denial, anger, bargaining with God, depression, and finally acceptance."[13]

We ought not to think that the stages which have been identified as preceding death come only at the end of a long life or before a sudden terminal illness. Throughout our lives each of us must come to terms with the denial of death. We must accept our angers at the termination of life and relationships which we cherish. We must overcome the depression which is an outgrowth of the fear of death. We must accept ourselves and our dying and death.

When we reflect on Karl Rahner's understanding of death we see that we are creatures who ache for the infinite. We are irrevocably spirit-matter. Therefore, our destiny must include both. When we accept death as that which gives fullest meaning to life and that which allows us the fullest personal expression, then we will be better able to understand that what happens after death is not cut off from life but is the fulfillment of life as we now know it. Heaven is truly our fulfillment and our destiny. For most Americans today, the image of a heaven filled with cherubin and seraphim is not palatable. As someone once asked, "What else is there to do in eternity besides saying 'Holy, holy, holy' forever?"

Rahner says that those who have died "live the unhampered and limitless life" of God.[14] Our destiny is to live in eternal bliss in the endless light of the beatific vision.

In 1336 Pope Benedict XII defined that this heavenly knowledge of God will be intuitive and face to face vision, without the mediation of any creature. *The divine essence, God himself, will show himself openly and clearly.* The blessed will take great joy in this experience of God; by it they will possess eternal life and peace.[15]

But is the beatific vision the fulfillment and destiny of the world today?

Americans today are acutely conscious of the evolutionary nature of the world. Day by day we are amazed with new scientific studies that reveal to us the wonders of our world. We are aware, consciously or not, that we are involved in a process of becoming.

People today live an evolutionary view of the world. They see themselves and mankind inescapably immersed in the current history. The world for them is not a static reality, but a world in the process of becoming.[16]

Rahner holds that the process of becoming in which we are involved is the "increasing divinization of the world."[18] We are involved in a journey of spirit and matter which was begun at creation. The destiny of this journey is the transfiguration of the universe. From the first moment of creation God gave himself in self-communication in the incarnation.

The free gift of God's grace, God's communication of himself was incorporated in the world from the beginning (. . .man as the goal of the world was intended by God from the start as man divinized). Consequently, world evolution really, and not merely in the divine "ideas," moves under the dynamism that is directed towards the "Kingdom of God."[17]

We understand evolution as a development from a lower state of being to a higher state. According to Rahner, then, the evolution of the world is the process of the transformation and transcending of matter toward spiritual and personal fulfillment. All of creation is developing toward that which is higher. This higher point of being is in fact the risen, cosmic Christ.

The history of nature and the world becomes the history of salvation and revelation. . . . Its "omega point" is in fact Christ, in whom created matter, finite spirit and the divine Logos, in whom all things subsist, are united in one person and this unity is manifested in history.[18]

Creation is heading toward an omega point which we call heaven. But heaven will not be an alien land. It is the destiny and fulfillment of all creation. This understanding of eternal life as the perfection and integration of created spirit and matter into final perfection challenges us as Americans.

For too long, our American attitude toward the material order has been one not only of neglect but often one of outright destruction. This is the negation of our very essence as human beings. We are finite spirit and matter. We have been created to be caretakers of the earth and the universe whose final destiny is part of our own fulfillment. The bishops of the United States remind us:

We have been created to share in the divine life through a destiny that goes far beyond our human capabilities and before which we must in all humility stand in awe. Like Mary in proclaiming her *Magnificat*, we marvel at the wonders God has done for us, how God has raised up the poor and the lowly and promised great things for them in the Kingdom. God now asks of us sacrifices and reflection on our reverence for human dignity—in ourselves and in others—and on our service and discipleship, so that the divine goal for the human family and this earth can be fulfilled. Communion with God, sharing God's life, involves a mutual bonding with all on this globe. Jesus taught us to love God and one another, and that the concept of neighbor is without limit. We know that we are called to be members of a new covenant of love. We have to move from our devotion to independence, to a commitment to human solidarity. That challenge must find its realization in the kind of community we build among us. Love implies concern for all—especially the poor—and a continued search for those social and economic structures that permit everyone to share in a community that is a part of a redeemed creation (Rom 8:21–23).[19]

Creation has already been redeemed. It was in the light of this understanding that Rahner not only theologized about death, he prayed about it. Rahner prayed:

Come! Come to us, You who never pass away, You whose day has no evening, whose reality knows no end! Come to us, because our reality is only a procession to the grave.

We have called out to your infinity—its coming is the sole hope we have of attaining unending life.

You took upon Yourself our kind of life, just as it is. You let it slip away from You, just as ours vanishes from us.

Is our grief taken from us, simply because You wept too? Is our surrender to finiteness no longer a terrible act of despair, simply because You also capitulated? Does our road, which doesn't want to end, have a happy ending despite itself, just because You are traveling it with us?

Slowly a light is beginning to dawn. I'm beginning to understand something I have known for a long time: You are still in the process of Your coming.

You are still coming. From Your Incarnation to the end of this era is only an instant, even though millennia may elapse and, being blessed by You, pass on to become a small part of this instant.

You must continue to come more and more. What has already taken place in the roots of all reality must be made more and more apparent. The false appearance of our world, the shabby pretense that it has not been liberated from finiteness through your assuming finiteness into Your own life, must be more and more thoroughly rooted out and destroyed.

O God who is to come, grant me the grace to live now, in the hour of your Advent, in such a way that I may merit to live in You forever, in the blissful hour of Your Eternity.[20]

We have examined Karl Rahner's theology of death and life after death. May Rahner's insights help us to pray in the face of our approaching death, "Come, Lord Jesus!" May Rahner's reflections help us to see that life passes through death into the limitless life of God. May we too pray, as Rahner did, that we will achieve our final destiny and live in God forever.

NOTES

1. David E. Stannard, *The Puritan Way of Death. A Study in Religion, Culture, and Social Change* (New York: Oxford University Press, 1977), p. 41.

2. Cited in *The Puritan Way of Death*, ibid. p. 81.

3. Ibid., pp. 155–156.

4. Jessica Mitford, *The American Way of Death* (New York: Simon and Schuster, 1963).

5. Karl Rahner, *Encounters with Silence* (Maryland: Christian Classics, 1984), p. 55.

6. Karl Rahner, "Death" *Sacramentum Mundi: An Encyclopedia of Theology*, Vol. 2 (New York: Herder and Herder, 1968), p. 58.

7. Ibid.

8. Ibid., p. 59.

9. Ibid.

10. Ibid., p. 60.

11. Ibid., p. 62.

12. Ibid.

13. "Sharing the Light of Faith," *National Catechetical Directory for Catholics of the United States* (Washington, D.C.: NCCB, 1977), #186.

14. *Encounters with Silence*, op. cit., p. 57

15. Germain Grisez, *The Way of the Lord Jesus Christ: Christian Moral Principles* (Chicago: Franciscan Herald Press, 1983), p. 464.

16. Karl Rahner, "Incarnation," *Sacramentum Mundi*, Vol. 3, op. cit., p. 117.

17. *Sacramentum Mundi*, Vol. 2, op. cit., p. 291.

18. Ibid.

19. *Economic Justice for All* (Washington, D.C.: NCCB, 1986), #365

20. Rahner, *Encounters with Silence*, (op. cit., pp. 81–87, passim.

Glossary

Absolute future—the final destiny of all creation which is God.

All-cosmic dimension of the soul—the permanent relationship of the soul with the ground of unity of the material order which has been assumed by Christ.

Beatific vision—the intuitive and face to face vision of God, without the mediation of any creature.

Concupiscence—disintegration we experience in our hearts, our lives, and in our relationships with God and others which is the result of sin.

Death—while clinical death is defined as the cessation of all biological functions, the exact moment of physical death is still strongly debated by physicians and scientists. Theologically death is the definitive self-surrender and final decision made by a person for or against God.

Eschatology—the study of the final events of human life and of the world, teachings on death and life after death. Eschatology may be presented from the perspective of events which will only happen in the future. This is called futuristic eschatology. It may also be presented from the perspective of events which have already taken place and have determined the final outcome. This is called realized eschatology.

General Judgment—the relationship of all individuals to the collective history of humankind and its destiny.

Hell—that state in which a person becomes the antithesis of what it means to be human.

Human beings—are made up of spirit and matter, capable of knowing what they experience through their senses and possessing a dynamic drive toward the infinite.

Incarnation—the second person of the Blessed Trinity became flesh and became a part of the human reality.

Millennialism—the belief that Christ will reign for a thousand years. Pre-millennialism holds that the thousand year reign will begin after the second coming of Christ. Post-millennialism holds that the reign is already in progress and that Christ will return at the end of a thousand years.

Particular Judgment—the presence of the word of God as the center of human existence as the standard by which individuals judge themselves.

Purgatory—the integration and harmonization of the individual with himself or herself, the world, and the universe which has been transformed by Christ.

Resurrection—the final perfection and fullfillment of human beings.

Second coming of Christ—the full manifestation of the transformation of creation by Christ.

Soul—that which gives the body life.

Supernatural existential—the demand or capacity of all creation for the supernatural.

Vorgrift—a dynamic drive in human beings which reaches out toward the infinite.

8398